TURNING POINTS

TURNING POINTS

The Memoirs
of Lord Wolfenden

THE BODLEY HEAD
LONDON SYDNEY
TORONTO

To my wife
who has shared all of it

© John Wolfenden 1976
ISBN 0 370 10442 0
Printed and bound in Great Britain for
The Bodley Head Ltd
9 Bow Street, London WC2E 7AL
by Redwood Burn Limited
Trowbridge and Esher
Set in Monotype Bembo
by Gloucester Typesetting Co Ltd
First published 1976

CONTENTS

ILLUSTRATIONS

PREFACE

I have never kept a diary, I have never hoarded private correspondence, and I have never regarded official memoranda as my personal property. Nor have I a very strong chronological sense. So there may well be inaccuracies of fact in what follows. If there are, I am sorry, but not devastated or deeply ashamed. This is intended as a personal recollection of events in which I happen to have been involved, not as documentation for the use of serious historians.

For the same reason the style is as informal and conversational as is compatible with the normal usages of grammar and syntax. My ambition is what I believe is called 'person-to-person communication'; and it is on that level that I would ask to be judged.

ACKNOWLEDGMENTS

Many people have helped me, in conversation and reminiscence. I would express particular thanks to Miss Jean Felton, Mr Michael Holton and Mr J. F. Johnson, who have refreshed my memory, and corrected my mis-memories, of the University Grants Committee, the Carnegie United Kingdom Trust and the University of Reading respectively. They are not, of course, responsible for my opinions or for mistakes of fact which may remain. Especially I am indebted to Elizabeth Eade for translating my handwriting into legible typescript with such accuracy, speed and good humour.

Thanks are due to the following for permission to reproduce copyright illustrative material: LNA Photos Ltd, facing page 161 (*bottom*); British Tourist Authority, facing page 161 (*top*); *Punch*, facing page 145 (*top and bottom*); Rex Coleman, jacket.

1

Return to Yorkshire
[1912]

The first turning point was when we went back to live in Yorkshire. For generations Wolfendens had lived up on the Lancashire border, in the valleys of the Calder and the Ryburn, slopping over sometimes down the other side of the Pennines into Burnley or Rochdale.

I had myself been born on the edge of Swindon, in Wiltshire, where my father had gone, daringly breaking away from a close-knit family of seven children to make his own way in the South. He was Registrar of the Swindon Technical College, and was obviously flourishing. But the ancestral pull was too strong, and he returned to the West Riding to a job in the Education Department at the County Hall in Wakefield. He stayed there for the rest of his life, moving steadily up the office ladder, increasingly respected and trusted, inside the building and throughout the education service, until his retirement. The old-time non-graduate 'Chief Clerk' is rapidly disappearing, and the education service is the poorer. His was a remarkable career for a boy who left school at twelve to become a 'part-timer'. And he was a remarkable man, in a quiet, soft-spoken, God-fearing way. He had his flashes of temper, but his family, his work, and his chapel were his full life. Later on he made something of a name as a writer of short stories in West Yorkshire dialect, dialogues of sentiment and philosophy between villagers dropping in on the clogger's shop – in its particular village the sober Nonconformist club, by contrast with the innocent but suspect bucolic abandon of the village pub.

My mother was very different. I never knew her parents – they died before I was born – but I knew her two brothers and her younger sister. That grandfather had had a greengrocer's shop in a suburb of

9

Halifax, and one of my uncles was reputed to have been the long-jump champion of Yorkshire. My mother was, I later came to realise, pretty, elegant and tasteful. She dressed very well, on what must have been minute expenditure, and later on became a typical member of the 'morning-coffee set' in the best Wakefield café. She certainly had what were called social ambitions, and she was sensitive enough to model her behaviour accordingly. My father never ceased to be proud of her. I doubt if she enjoyed the return to Yorkshire as much as he did.

For me, of course, it was not a return. At the age of six I had seldom been to the West Riding; it was a long way from Swindon and railway fares could not be afforded very often. But at the age of six one takes what comes, whether it be the loss of a younger brother who died of meningitis when I was five and he was four, or the first sight of a flying-machine or the news of the sinking of the *Titanic*. (The first public event I remember is the death of King Edward VII when I was four : I could not understand why the newspaper on a particular day had a thick black line round the pages.) So I went along, with no emotion that I can remember, still less with any realisation that this was a turning point.

In Wakefield we lived on the very edge of the town, as we had done in Swindon. The house had the surprising title *Alpha Cottage* carved on a stone set into its front wall. Perhaps it had been the first house to be built on that road; by the time we knew it it had become, as 196 Alverthorpe Road, one of a terrace, itself standing just at the point where terrace houses in the ordinary sense gave way to two or three 'better class' dwellings, culminating in the doctor's house at the top of the rise. It was not anything like a cottage. There were four imposing steps up to the front door (and therefore a commodious coal-cellar) and a hall from which opened a bleak 'front room', and a broad staircase went upstairs. At the back was a living-room and a kitchen-scullery, with steps down to the cellar. The front garden consisted of a dreary row of laurel bushes and a narrow bed of unenthusiastic lilies of the valley; the back garden had one small square of grass, a lilac tree and an abutting wall of the house next door which later became useful for elementary tennis practice. My parents, naturally, had the front bedroom and I the back one. The only disadvantage of that was that on their way to bed they passed my door and could catch me reading in bed, either by candlelight or by a torch hidden under the bedclothes. The first sound I heard in the mornings was the 'click-sperlosh' as the *Yorkshire Post* and the *Daily News* flipped up the leather flap on the back door and splashed over the living-room linoleum. Meals, homework, domestic mending all took mutually competitive place in the living-room. The dining-table was never uncovered, except for rare games of ping-pong; this was before the days of 'table-tennis', and the bats made the right onomatopoeic noise. It was perhaps as well that we had no need to accommodate radio and television as well.

I suppose, in retrospect, I had very few friends of my own age. I was strongly discouraged from playing with the children lower down the road, much as I envied their noisy cricket on an adjacent abandoned brick-field; and we lived too far from the centre of the town for random excursions into it. I missed, from Swindon, the evolutions of the Yeomanry on their exercise ground behind the house, and the neighbourly interchange of impromptu games in the long gardens, and the cattle-market, and the corncrakes in the field at the end of the road. But open country was only a few hundred yards away; and there were nests in the hedges, newts in the ponds and larks in the sky.

In Swindon I had attended a dame's school. It was the genuine and authentic article, conducted for eight or ten of us by two maiden ladies in a shed at the bottom of their garden in one of the best parts of Swindon. Heaven knows what their qualifications were, or how I came to go there. What I do remember is being taught the elements of English grammar and the necessity for correct spelling: *o si sic omnes*! The fact that I chewed off the corners of the grammar book may well have some sinister esoteric explanation: the taste of the resulting juice remains.

To be pitchforked from this into a Church of England elementary school in Wakefield might have been traumatic – perhaps it was, in ways of which I am not conscious. I had never before been in a class-room, with thirty-five other boys and girls, seated with due sex segregation, or attended a singing lesson when two or three classes were brigaded (not to say dragooned) together. I had never lined up in due order, standing on a marked spot on the assembly hall floor, for morning prayers at the beginning of the day. Still less had I ever recited the Apostles' Creed. For generations we had been Methodists (Wesleyan, not Primitive) and all my grandparents' sons were Chapel

Stewards or Circuit Stewards or local preachers. The eldest had a dazzling reputation as a 'boy preacher' and to the end of his days tramped the hills preaching twice a Sunday to enthusiastic congregations. So what I was doing in a Church school I never knew. I suspect now that it may have been because this particular school had a high reputation for achieving free places at the Grammar School. Whatever the reason, the public recitation of the Apostles' Creed, thitherto to me wholly unheard of, added to all the other embarrassing novelties.

For I was a freak. Chiefly because my contemporaries and I could not understand each other's manner of speech. I spoke with the Southern long 'a' and short 'u': they the opposite. This had never been a problem for me with the older generation; it had seemed quite natural that that should be their pronunciation; and my parents had had the gumption (long 'u') to adapt their speech to that of their neighbours in Swindon. But here I was in a classroom, in a minority of one, talking lah-di-dah, decades before the BBC had brought 'standard English' into every home in the land. Ridicule, of course, is the standard weapon of the young against the unfamiliar, and when they were in a majority of thirty-five to one they were not sparing in their use of it. Sometimes there were hot tears at the end of the day. But there were some sympathetic teachers, and even the terrifying Headmistress, armed with a strap which was not carried merely for ornament, seemed to recognise that there was somebody here who needed to be shielded rather than shouted at.

Anyhow, it did not last long. After a few months I was mysteriously transferred, under age, to the Junior School of the Grammar School. And there I spent ten years revelling (usually) in what I still believe to be one of the best kinds of education in the world.

One enormous advantage of the return to Yorkshire was seeing more of the paternal grandparents and the uncles and aunts. From Wakefield to Sowerby Bridge, on the old L & Y, was an easy through journey, and then there was a motor-train or a tram from Sowerby Bridge to Triangle, where they lived. Their house was unusual. It was in a terrace, set back and up from the road, back-to-back with the next street up the hillside, but one storey below the back terrace, because of the slope. You went in through a door in the wall at road level, up a dozen steps, to a small square flagged garden, on the ground-floor level of the house, with a view straight across the valley to the opposite hillside. Inside the front door the stairs went straight up to the higher floors; immediately on your right on the ground floor was the living-room. It had a vast fireplace, with an oven on one side and on the other a hot-water tank filled from a tap and emptied by jugful through the top. There was, of course, a grandfather clock, complete with smiling moon, and a sombre religious picture almost filling the side opposite the window on to the garden. There was also, significantly, a bookcase. On the first floor was the sitting-room, hardly ever used except either when one of the family was courting, which happened very seldom, or when music was being made, which happened very often. The elder daughter was a soprano star of the Halifax Amateur Operatic Society, and for weeks before the annual *Samson and Delilah* or *Gondoliers* the room, indeed the whole house, rang with her practising. One of the sons played the violin, and after he was married regularly came back to play duets with one of the sisters. The Welsh seem to think they have a monopoly of singing. There was more of it in that one Yorkshire valley than in all the valleys of South Wales put together. Everybody, but everybody, could go straight on if you gave them a couple of bars anywhere in 'T'Messiah'.

The main pieces of furniture in the sitting-room were a grand piano and two murky oleographs, one on each side of the massive fireplace. They represented, predictably, John Bright and William Ewart Gladstone. On the next floor were bedrooms and then a capacious attic with two beds, in one of which I always slept, to be awakened in the winter dark by the clatter of clogs on the cobbles as the shawled mill-girls answered the summons of the hooter. Here too were books, including an ancient many-volumed encyclopedia which I read endlessly by candlelight since there was no gas on that floor. All in all, climate and context apart, the house, in shape and size, was remarkably similar to the Director's Residence in the British Museum.

For me personally one of the major joys was long walks with my grandfather. He was a short stocky man with bow legs and a bald head. He worked in the Co-op flour-mill in Sowerby Bridge. What he did I never precisely knew, but sometimes he 'worked nights', taking his jock-'ankersch', that is, his overnight food wrapped in a red and white handkerchief, with him on an evening tram. Then, after he got up next day, he would take me out with him up on to the high meadows and the moors. He taught me to recognise a lapwing or peewit (but he called it a teewite) and the flocks of starlings in the autumn (but they were shepsters) and how to find a skylark's nest, but in no circumstances to disturb it. We picked pint after pint of bilberries. I have no recollection of any conversation. None was necessary, and he was a silent, self-contained man. On his deathbed, years later, when I was an undergraduate, he said to me that he did not know how 'this job' was going to end, but that there was something for me in his jacket pocket across the room, and perhaps I would like to buy something with it. It was a ten-shilling note, riches beyond price. He would have been slightly surprised if he had known that I bought Roger Fry's *Vision and Design*, but he wouldn't have said anything.

My grandmother was a Roman matron born out of time and place. She had strong features, a decisive judgment and a firm manner with her children. When two middle-aged sons exceeded the permitted level of noise and combativeness in political argument she would cut in with 'Stop your fratching,' and they stopped. If a hard-luck story was produced as an excuse for some minor failure she would say, 'He mud 'a knooan better.' She was certainly not sour or heartless; but she was stern, and bringing up seven children had led her towards realism rather than sentiment. She had been born a Howarth – it might have been Hoyle, or Whiteley, or Sutcliffe or Barrett, the other surnames which were intermingled with ours – and her brother was the farmer who brought the daily milk, in a shining can with the measures hanging and rattling on a curving bar inside. It was whispered that he enjoyed a drop of something stronger than milk at some of the houses where he called on his morning round: his sister gave him strong tea.

She and her husband both read the printed word with difficulty. The *British Weekly* and the *Halifax Weekly Courier* lasted them the week. But their ambitions for their children were limitless. The eldest, the dazzling boy preacher, died a bachelor, after a rolling-stone life as postman, poultry farmer, smallholder and, most notably, clogger. He presided over the clogger's-shop club which provided the background for my father's dialect stories. It was a dark low first-floor room with windows on one side overlooking the cobbled village street and on the other looking on to his hen-run. With his mouth full of nails he hammered away, with the flat of a file, at boots or clogs. Conversation had to be either very loud or nicely timed to fit the gaps in his hammering; but it never wholly stopped. It was there that I first heard pronouncements about Free Trade, short time in the mills, and the wickednesses of the Church of England. The second son held local trade union office; the third was my father; the fourth was, to the end of his days, cashier in a local mill; the youngest went to be a bank clerk in London. The two girls, who came fourth and sixth, were both elementary school teachers, the younger college-trained, the elder not. The eldest son and the two daughters lived at home, so there was a reasonable amount of money coming in to the house. Being in debt was mortal sin: the road to salvation was the weekly payment to the Building Society, though its apportionment between the three of them seemed to create more friction than goodwill.

I have said that we were Methodists. Chapel on Sunday was the weekly gathering of the family. Wherever they had been, or whatever they had been doing through the week, on Sunday the whole family was united in the worship of God. It was a long walk, even by adult measurements, a full two miles each way, uphill most of the way there but mercifully downhill back. Some walked faster than others; but nobody waited for anybody else; and sometimes the late-comers arrived during the first hymn – but never later than that. The whole family sat together in a vast pew at the very back; there were footstools, and a hanging box to hold the Bibles and hymn-books. It was a massive building, substantial inside and out. The choir faced the congregation, above the open pulpit, and we sang our hymns as if to command the special attention of the Almighty, not shouting at Him but using the very tops of the voices with which He had endowed us. Pew discipline was strict. My prime duty was to be quiet – except, of course, during the hymns. I was permitted to follow the reading of the lessons in a pew Bible. If the sermon was above my head or too long for juvenile endurance, again I was allowed to read the Bible, provided that I kept quiet and did not ask questions.

Those sermons were quite something. It was a remote hillside chapel and it was not more than once a month that a minister came – and there were agonising problems of hospitality when he did. So seven out of eight sermons were preached by local preachers, chosen from a panel organised by the circuit. I have no doubt that discreet and godly popularity polls took place, and it was a matter of deep concern, when the quarterly list of preachers' engagements appeared, to see which ones each chapel had been allotted. These local preachers were extraordinary men. Unlettered, uneducated, wholly unacademic, farmers, shop-keepers, house-painters, mill-hands, they had the heart of the matter in them: they had something to say, and they said it, in language understanded of the people. Some of them attended the Mutual Improvement Societies, our rural equivalent of the Mechanics' Institutes of the towns. Most of them spent practically all their leisure time preparing their sermons, and themselves, for Sunday, and for their appearance before devout but highly critical congregations. The trade union movement had solid foundations in those who preached, and those who listened, in these unpretentious places of devout worship.

As we poured out of chapel, the weekly gossip session began. It was the only time in the week when most of the congregation met each other or spoke to each other, communications being what they then were. Most of the talk was about health – or rather, about illness, about each other's old people, children, grandchildren. Sometimes there were administrative problems to discuss, about who was going to provide the tea at next week's Sale of Work or the route of the farm-cart which was to collect for the Jumble Sale. For a visiting grandchild this was all totally boring. Besides, he was getting hungry, and there were those two miles, albeit downhill, still to be traversed.

But when you did get back home, my goodness, it was worth it. Again the whole family was present, unless something very unusual called one of them away. The first course was, gloriously, Yorkshire pudding, served as it should be, all by itself swimming in gravy on a hot plate. The sophisticated will say that this was to take the edge off the appetite. No: it was to permit full enjoyment of something which if it is properly made (and, of course, it was) deserves concentrated and undivided attention. Then the joint, carved by the eldest male present – Grandfather always excepted; he said he was too slow. It all took some time, and in those circles in those days it was not considered unmannerly to comment on the quality of the food. And always a good sustaining pudding. It was, in fact, the weekly blow-out, with the added spice of exchange of information about what had been happening to everybody during the past week.

Sunday afternoon was not a very active time. But revival came with a cup of strong tea at five o'clock, to fortify us for the day's second two-mile walk to chapel.

But for me these were luxury jaunts, at half-term or in school holidays. The solid part of life was school. I was no longer quite such a freak linguistically as I had been at the elementary school. Now, in the Junior School of the Grammar School, there were mistresses and masters who spoke in the same way as I did. And so did a high proportion of the boys. The Junior School had a separate Headmaster, form mistresses for the two lower forms, and form masters for the two higher ones. By enlightened timetabling it also had masters from the Senior School for specialist subjects like history, geography and Divinity (as it was then called). So from an early age mature standards of accuracy and scholarship were learnt. The Headmaster was a burly man, who had a language of his own in class and the gentleness of a giant when he played football with us. Year by year we mounted from I Lower to II Upper, and by then we were due for transfer to the Senior School, where we should join the standard intake of fee-payers and 'scholarship boys'.

In my last year in the Junior School the Senior School had a new Headmaster, and it was my duty, duly primed, to call for three cheers for him at the end of his first visit to the Junior School. It was not quite clear to me, unfamiliar with the habits of these Olympians, exactly when his address to us was ended, and he was out of the door and into the passage before I collected myself to make my first (and briefest) public speech. He came back into the room and made a characteristically affable reply: but I was roasted by my own Headmaster for stupidly missing my cue.

I was allowed to skip the Third Form and landed in IVA. This had significance, because that was where it was possible to begin to add Greek to the Latin we had already started. It was also the place where academic competition really began. Three streams flowed together; the minority who had come up from the Junior School, all of us paying fees but some, like me, assisted by Foundation Scholarships awarded by the Governors, the fee-payers who had come up from the Third Forms and the boys who had come from the elementary schools with scholarships awarded by the local education authority. Academically we were more or less homogeneous: in other respects we were very different, socially, financially and linguistically. The doctor's son and the solicitor's son spoke the same way as I did, though their fathers were far better off than mine. The scholarship boys for the most part used the short 'a' and the long 'u' to which I had become accustomed but could never bring myself to utter. What we all had in common was what it sounds priggish to call a genuine desire to learn and to 'get on'. This is not the place for educational dogma or sociological theorising: but from my experience of it I cannot imagine a better instrument for social mixing or social mobility than a good day grammar school in the North of England at the beginning of this century.

Our eagerness to 'get on' did not necessarily make us well-behaved in the classroom. We were by now well into the First World War, and that had already had grave effects on staffing. Most of those who taught us were either excluded from the Forces by physical unfitness or retired schoolmasters who had nobly come back to 'do their bit'. To one of these latter we were particularly cruel, not because he was unreasonable to us or because, given the chance, he could not teach, but just because he was so helpless in the face of twenty-five vigorous and ebullient schoolboys. He was quite incapable of keeping us in order and it did not take long for minor acts of disobedience to mount into total chaos. Our form-room, luckily for us and unluckily for him, was at the opposite end of the building from the Headmaster's own room, so our misbehaviour went unnoticed for some time. But one day the Headmaster passed the door on his way to the Junior School and could not fail to hear the uproar. He burst in, flaming with fury, gave us the dressing-down of all time, with pointed pungencies about inconsiderate, ungentlemanly and heartless behaviour, and left us in no doubt either about what he thought of us or about what would happen to us if he heard a murmur from us again. I learnt then for the first time that there are some people in this world, certainly in the academic world, who are just 'bully-fodder'. It seems not to matter how clever they are, or how generous; there simply is something about them which makes it impossible for them to stand up to a classroom full of boys, or, for that matter, to their colleagues. I also learnt the full impact of a blazingly angry headmaster. I suppose he lost his temper, as he had every excuse for doing. But it may have been that he just pretended to. It is no bad thing for a headmaster to pretend to lose his temper now and then.

November the eleventh 1918 was, naturally, a rather unusual day. We had been told that if the Armistice was duly signed the Union Jack would be broken over the Town Hall at eleven o'clock. It happened that from where I sat in the Lower Fifth Form classroom I could see the flagstaff on the Town Hall. The poor man who was trying to teach us Latin composition had a miserable half-hour as the hands of the clock climbed with unspeakable slowness towards eleven o'clock. Then came maroons, church bells, cheers. I yelled 'There it is!' as the flag mounted its staff. And we all roared out into the streets and added our own uninhibited row to the pandemonium going on all round us. It was not until afterwards that I learnt that my youngest uncle, a bank clerk in peacetime, had died of pneumonia in Boulogne at ten o'clock that morning.

So, form by form, year by year, *pedetemptim progredientes*, we approached the hurdles for which we had been schooled, the external examinations. Wakefield, like its sister grammar schools at Leeds and Bradford, had a formidable reputation in these matters; and if it would be exaggeration to say that it was as important to beat them in the Oxford Locals results as it was to beat them at football and cricket, there was nevertheless a feeling that corporate as well as individual reputations were involved. In this year, 1920, we did reasonably well. Indeed, we were told, more as a threat than as a promise, that we were a good year and that much was expected of us in the future.

The school year after the first public examination was expected to have a degree of leisure about it. After all, the next one was two years off, and we could surely be allowed to relax a bit and pace ourselves for this longer course. Anything but. The masters who were responsible for the Lower Sixth knew all about this temptation, and they fought as for our souls. By now we were a small form. Specialisation had deepened, and not more than half a dozen of us survived into the Classical Lower Sixth. For some subjects, Greek Testament, Latin translation, Greek plays and Ancient History, we were taken jointly with the two years of the Classical Upper Sixth. We read their set books, and although we were not expected to know the footnotes as thoroughly as they were we had to try to hold our own with them in knowledge and translation of the actual texts.

I doubt if it ever occurred to us to wonder about, still less to criticise, the 'hideous over-specialisation', as some would call it, which our week's work represented. I learnt no German, very little French, no mathematics, no science, from the age of fourteen onwards. This has, I know, been a lifelong deprivation. But it would be quite wrong to suppose that we did nothing but Latin and Greek and Ancient History. Those were the three subjects we were 'taking' for the next hurdle, the Higher Certificate Examination. But critics who look no further than a syllabus omit one very important factor from the educational equation – the teachers. Here, at that school at that time, we were abundantly fortunate.

Really there were three who mattered. The Classical Sixth form master was tall, awkward, short-sighted, with a mouthful of teeth. He talked rapidly, almost incessantly, and always provocatively. He was suspected of holding political views just a shade to the left of centre. He opened up, in English lessons, the whole new world (as it then was) of modern plays, Shaw, Ibsen, Flecker, the lot. Anything, anywhere, in Euripides or in that morning's paper, would trigger off an argument about politics or religion or economics, until the whole lot of us were shouting at the tops of our voices, all at once, to the often-expressed disgust of some more pedestrian pedagogue who was trying to make himself heard in the room opposite. I suppose it was in these unruly disputations that my interest in philosophy was born, though I was far from realising it at the time.

The second was one of the 'wartime dug-outs', a man, I guess, then well on in his sixties. He was not an orthodox professional schoolmaster. He deliberately cultivated mystery about himself; he lived alone in a hotel in the town, where he sometimes invited senior boys to visit him; he had played cricket for a minor county; he was thought to be socially a cut above most of his colleagues; and either behind a cricket net or in a classroom his most usual form of speech was a rasping grunt. He took us for Ancient History. He had, he frankly told us, never studied the subject, either at school or at the university. But he had a close friend who was an Ancient History don at Oxford. This unselfish scholar provided his own lecture notes, which were solemnly, and intelligently, dictated for us to take down. If our mentor was uncertain about anything, or if we raised questions which he could not answer, letters flew between Wakefield and Oxford until all was made plain. It all sounds quite ludicrous, and so, by any standards of modern enlightened teaching, it was. But it worked – and not just from the point of view of examination results. We were in fact getting university-level teaching from the age of fifteen onwards, transmitted, it is true, through channels not of the deepest or clearest; but nobody ever took more trouble with any class anywhere than this totally unprofessional 'temporary'; above all, he never pretended.

The most memorable of the three was the Headmaster himself, Alfred John Spilsbury. He was what is called, sometimes with a slightly patronising air, 'a born schoolmaster'. He was essentially a Londoner, and had probably never been north of the Trent until he came, in his early forties, to be Headmaster of a totally Yorkshire day school. He belonged to a different world, but he took immense pains to adapt himself to what he secretly regarded as the barbarians of the North. He joined the Rotary Club, took morning coffee in the town (and was frequently late for the Classical Upper Sixth in consequence), gave tennis parties, at which senior boys learnt to play mixed doubles with wives of School Governors, and generally spread what he would in private have called 'sweetness and light'. But primarily he was a schoolmaster, and a dedicated Classic. My first classroom encounter with him had been when he tried to make a Fourth Form treat Latin as a living language. As a disciple of W. H. D. Rouse he engaged us in conversation in Latin and wrote it all up on the blackboard. We thought it was all a bit mad but, after all, he was Headmaster and we had to humour him and if that was how he liked it who were we to spoil his fun? Later on, we heard him sing the choruses of Sophocles, prancing round the room in time, more or less, to his intonings. Remember that this was fifty years ago, and in those days, to put it mildly, unconventional.

But he brought more to us than lively teaching. He refereed football matches, vocally; he played Eton fives with us, carefully; he conducted school prayers, militarily; and he taught us to play billiards on his miniature table, hospitably. He did not 'take' on everybody. Some of his Governors thought he was not exacting enough; some of his staff thought he was too libertarian; some of the boys thought he was sloppy. But to some of us he represented what we were beginning to see existed outside Wakefield, a world where scholarly and social graces were valued for their own sake, apart from the necessities of daily toil and money.

For me personally he had the added attribute of being the father of three daughters. The eldest, Clytie, was of my own age, the next, Eileen, a couple of years younger, and the third, Rohais, five years younger than that. They, or some of them, would from time to time come and watch us as we played fives or tennis with their father. Somehow two or three of us came gradually to speaking terms. And for an only child, as I then was, this imperceptibly became a quasi-family relationship. He and his wife seemed to think that the girls might do worse, in their unaccustomed northern environment, than get to know some of the more presentable of the natives. So after fives or tennis we were invited to stay to tea, and as sixteen-year-old bachelors began to learn how to behave.

The whole family background was totally different from mine. The Headmaster's house had rooms vastly bigger than ours, with furniture and pictures of a kind I had never seen before. He himself, on his mother's side, came from one of the historic families of Guernsey, which explains why all his children carried the name Le Messurier. Left early an orphan he had distinguished himself at Christ's Hospital and at the Oxford college to which he steered me; and although there was never much money there was an atmosphere of taken-for-granted interest in scholarship, literature, music and the theatre. His wife was, for Wakefield, exotic. Her mother had been a Lancashire lass, but her father was a Russian from Odessa, of whom family tradition relates that he stood on a hill and watched the charge of the Light Brigade at Balaclava. She herself, much the youngest in her family, was brought up in France and then came to England to work as a secretary in Oxford. Her speech was never wholly tamed to English pronunciation, and there was a genuine cosmopolitanism in her views and her expression of them which was, to say the least, unusual in the wives of Yorkshire grammar school headmasters in the 1920s. My parents were laconic, she was voluble; they concealed their feelings, she expressed hers with vividness and warmth; they wrote letters with difficulty, hers flowed irrepressibly on, in a beautiful hand. Every time I went through the Headmaster's front door I went into a new and exciting world.

The three girls all went to the local High School, our sister foundation. Their walk, from the Headmaster's house to their school, was a few hundred yards. Mine, from precisely the opposite direction, was a good mile and a half. So it was a matter of rather exact timing to ensure that I met them, on our respective ways, each morning. If I did, nothing happened except that they smiled and I raised my school cap: if I did not, the day had got off to a bad start. For the record, it may as well be admitted here and now that ten years later the middle one and I were married and lived happily ever after.

The School teams during this period were very good indeed. I had to say a premature farewell to the Rugger XV as a result of injury. The cartilage in my right knee slipped as I turned to catch the ball on a slippery ground, and while the knee was out the whole of the opposing pack came and sat on it. That might still have been all right if I had not, after touch-line treatment, returned to the game and had the same thing happen again a few minutes later. That meant good-bye to the best game in the world, and a retirement to more sedate occupations like touch-judging and, later, goal-keeping at other games. Cricket was still possible, but, frankly, never as enjoyable as the physical clash of the fifteen-a-side game. Nor were we quite as formidable at this game as at the other. I suspect that the real reason was that the wickets we played on, especially (where it is most important) in the nets, were not reliable, so that if you played the stroke you ought to play you were more likely than not to be caught in the slips. Perhaps it was the unreliability of the wickets that usually produced a result in short one-day matches. Occasionally we had the luxury of a twelve o'clock start, not in school matches but in games against club sides like the Yorkshire Gentlemen or the Craven Gentlemen, and these brought our first opportunities for exercising adult lunch-time hospitality in a strange long low room underneath the groundsman's house.

The Headmaster and his family continued my social education. Their practice, in the Easter and summer holidays, was to take a cottage, either in the Yorkshire Dales or by the sea north of Whitby, and fill it with their older friends, with boarders from their School House whose parents were abroad, and sometimes with oddments like me. Walking miles and miles in Wensleydale and Waldendale and Swaledale was not unlike walking with my grandfather over the Sowerby moors. Certainly it produced an affection for that part of the country which has never died; and when anybody enthuses about some piece of Britain our stock question still is 'How does it compare with the top end of Swaledale?' One of the older friends, an adopted uncle, was a great bird-man – he looked very like a secretary bird himself – and a great map-reader; but he had no handy catalogue of the fields where bulls were, and detours were frequently necessary at certain times of the year. The seaside was less agreeable. I never did hold with total immersion in public; I was a poor swimmer; and I could never really trust my knee. The sea off the north-east coast of Yorkshire was unattractively cold, and there always seemed to be a howling gale. A fair amount of shivering agony was endured for the sake of keeping up appearances. The gales had their points, when thundering seas broke over the sea-wall and thumped against the cottage windows. I have never enjoyed, or trusted, the sea. One of the more comic of my later athletic achievements was a place in my College water-polo team. But that was in goal.

Time passed; and there loomed the biggest academic test of all. After three external examinations and three years in the Classical Sixth some of us were deemed ripe for university scholarship attempts. In those days it was very far from the case that acceptance by a university almost automatically carried with it the necessary funds. (Yes, I know that nowadays student grants are perennially inadequate: in those days it was competition, not qualification, that determined your income.) In one highly important particular we were very fortunate. Wakefield was one of some fifteen schools, all in the North of England, which were entitled to enter candidates for the awards made by Queen's College, Oxford, on the foundation of Lady Elizabeth Hastings. This admirable eighteenth-century Yorkshire woman had not only left a substantial sum of money for this purpose, but, with the aid of her spiritual adviser, had laid down in her will the most detailed instructions for the examination and selection of her beneficiaries. The rector of a named parish was to assemble the candidates and examine them in Greek, Latin and Hebrew, with the assistance of suitable academic coadjutors. Eventually, after appropriate eliminations, the names of twice as many candidates as there were awards were to be put into an urn and well shaken. Those whose names, up to the number of the awards, were first drawn from the urn were duly elected. This procedure the pious Lady Betty ordained 'as leaving something to Providence'. It is the origin of the deathless canard that Hastings Scholars were chosen by lot.

The conditions and circumstances had changed down the years. The examination was now set and marked by the College itself; Hebrew was no longer a requirement; the candidates attended not at Methley Rectory but at the University of Leeds; and, to the best of my knowledge and belief, the urn had been abandoned as an instrument of selection. The purist might say that these were technically 'close' awards. Yes, indeed, but closed to fifteen of the most academically-minded schools in the North of England. Further, they were for competition in all subjects, not just Classics, but History, Modern Languages, Science and Mathematics as well. Furthermore, the examination took place in November, before any of the Open Scholarship examinations at Oxford or Cambridge; so all the brightest and best from all those schools were candidates. Finally, the value of an award was a hundred pounds, whereas most Oxbridge Open Scholarships were eighty pounds; and that made an enormous difference.

The vast Great Hall of Leeds University was an intimidating setting, and the rows and rows of seemingly confident competitors were terrifying. Three Fellows of the College supervised the inquisition with patience, care and thoroughness, leaving their High Table and their tutorials for a week to enable the College to get its pick of the North and Lady Betty to rest quiet in her grave. One by one we were summoned to the dons' table to undergo personal interrogation. In those days schoolboys had a proper awe-ful respect for grave and reverend academic seniors, and our interviews did nothing to dispel it.

Eventually the examination was over. We had written all we knew (or could remember); we had done our best to guess the Unseens – one was a piece of Homer, written in a kind of Greek some of us had never seen before; we had tried to write an English essay which should be at the same time learned, elegant, well-informed and humorous; we had done our best to reproduce the rhythm of a Ciceronian sentence; and we had displayed our know-ledge of the stages of the constitutional development of the Athenian democracy. Now, drained, there was nothing to do but wait, until the Olympians at Queen's should decide whether or not they wanted us to join their stable. No: there was just one more thing we had to do. We had to prepare our entry forms for the forthcoming Oxford Open Scholarships, in case, as seemed likely, our names did not pop up out of the metaphorical urn. Somehow, it was automatically Oxford that we thought of, no doubt because the three masters with whom we had most to do all came from there. Cambridge was a fate worse than death, like Lancashire.

We waited, and our parents waited, more anxious than they let us see. One dark night there was a ring on the front door bell, an unusual event. My father left my mother and me in the living-room, lit the gaslight inside the front door and opened it. On the doorstep was the Headmaster, who had never been to the house before and must have had some difficulty in finding it. He said, with affected casualness, 'Oh, I just thought you might like to know that I've heard from Queen's this evening – he's got one.' Three of us had been candidates. Each of us had 'got one'. And that Headmaster had spent a foul winter evening tramping round miles and miles to each of three houses to let us know that night.

My parents did not say much, that night or ever. We were, after all, taciturn Yorkshire folk, not given to facile expression of our feelings. In fact, the deeper the feelings the less they were spoken. There might be a momentary trembling of a lip, or a sudden start of tears to the eye, or a quick pressure of the hand; but there were very few words, either in joy or in sorrow. I have no doubt that they were proud of my first major academic triumph. Oxford was to them as much a symbol as a reality. Neither of them had had any formal schooling worth mentioning, but they had a genuine respect for education even if they did not quite understand what it was all about. And they were totally committed to the view that if it were humanly possible I should have what they had not had. It was all part of an undemonstrative ambition for me and a vicarious self-fulfilment for themselves. It was a matter of course that in the evenings nothing interfered with my homework. My mother sewed while my father and I shared the table and worked. He always brought work home from the office, and spent the evening drafting letters or impatiently correcting the drafts of his subordinates; and neither he nor I would read anything else until we had finished our respective jobs. It may sound, by today's standards, rather bleak and joyless. It was not, because we all enjoyed what we were doing; and anyway we had no money to waste on frivolities. And it was certainly not priggish or precious, because it was perfectly natural and unassumed. They never expected or asked for any reward except the satisfaction of knowing that I was 'doing well', and the very last thing they would do would be to boast about it.

There was one pitfall about having an Oxford scholarship in the bag as early in the academic year as November. There was the whole of the rest of the school year to live through until the following July. In the 1970s there is no problem: there are VSO and CSV and any number of other ways of occupying, with pleasure and rapid increase in maturity, a God-given interval of six or nine months at that stage. Fifty years ago there were no such opportunities. One simply stayed on at school. It was, of course, *suave mari magno* as others tried to collect scholarships in one or other of the Oxford or Cambridge groups; and it was very *dulce desipere in loco*. But there was every inducement to make a mess of those last few months. With a certain amount of immodest self-esteem the editorship of the school magazine could become an invitation to self-display. With increasing flexibility in one's school timetable there was a temptation to do what one enjoyed and give the rest a miss. There was, fortunately as it turned out, another examination in the spring, for the Akroyd Scholarship, one only for the whole of Yorkshire in any subject, and for yet another attack on the Higher School Certificate for the purpose of amassing enough marks to add a City Major Scholarship. Yes, it took me three separate competitive examinations to collect enough money to face a university career without cost to my parents. So, with a few ups and a good many downs, the last summer of school life came. The climax, of course, was Speech Day, in a huge marquee on the playing-field behind the school. Bits of *Hamlet* were performed in a blazing afternoon's sunshine; some of us declaimed passages from Edmund Burke, John Stuart Mill and others. The Guest of Honour was that great Yorkshireman Sir Michael Sadler, then Vice-Chancellor of the University of Leeds, suave, pungent, civilised. As he handed to me Jowett's translation of Plato's *Republic* he asked, 'Have you read this already?' I replied, truthfully, 'No, sir.' 'My dear boy, I envy you if you have your first time of reading the *Republic* ahead of you.' There were many 'first times' ahead of me.

2

Queen's College, Oxford
[1924]

The first time I ever saw the dreaming spires was from the train which brought me to Oxford as a freshman in October 1924. Whereas practically everybody else had been to Oxford before either for scholarship examinations or for admission interviews we Northerners elected by lot on the foundation of Lady Elizabeth Hastings had been spared the expense of the journey – and we were not likely to have visited Oxford for any other reason.

I was, understandably but perhaps embarrassingly, 'romantic' about the whole thing. Not only was I a 'first-generation-university' type. More, the whole notion that a member of the family was going to Oxford was a paradisal dream come true, for parents, grandparents, uncles, aunts and cousins, even if they had no very clear idea what it meant. I myself had all the right naive pictures of it, based, I suppose, on *Sinister Street* and *Jude the Obscure*. There was more to it than that. This was the realisation of life's first major conscious ambition. It was the opening of the door to untold and unimagined riches, of the mind and of the spirit. Nowadays, going to university is almost routine for young men and women of a recognised degree of academic ability. In those days it was not; it was a highly competitive affair, and to have succeeded in getting there was both a personal triumph, with attendant self-esteem, and a promise of access to higher things. Yes, 'higher'. We were humbler then. Even the self-satisfaction at this achievement was a sign of humility. We were entering upon ground hitherto reserved for others than ourselves. In short, we believed ourselves to be entering upon something which was a privilege, not, as it is now widely regarded, a right. These sentiments must today seem obsolete, pathetic, ludicrous.

I can only say that they were ingenuously real for me and many like me in the 1920s.

If you had asked whether we thought the privilege to which we were being admitted was an academic one or a social one I think our reply would have been confused. We had not much doubt that we could hold our own academically with the Salopians and Rugbeians who were our contemporaries. (Queen's did not go in for Wyke-hamists, and Etonians, though they occurred, seemed to be rare birds who had touched down on an unintended spot in their migration up the Thames.) But we had every kind of doubt about the social part of it. And it may as well be confessed straight away that our intention was to conform to their behaviour and their values. This is no doubt shocking today. We ought, doubtless, to have invaded their social citadels, overthrown their altars and established the values and standards of the meritocracy. But in the first place we were not revolutionaries; we were aspirants to conformity. Secondly, we did not know that we were a meritocracy. Nobody had told us – and anyway, the word had not then been invented.

I suppose the first outward and visible sign was the pattern of the ordinary term-time day. We were essentially day-boys, and the working day had been shaped accordingly, with due regard for the 'train-boys' who came from anywhere within a radius of fifteen miles. So we had had four periods of teaching in the morning, and two in the afternoon, except that there was no school on Wednesday and Saturday afternoons. Then, and only then, we played our games. On full school days we knocked off at four o'clock and went home to the necessary hours of homework. Now we had to get used to a different rhythm. Lectures occurred at hourly intervals from nine o'clock onwards – though nobody in his right mind would have dreamt of attending, still less giving, them at the ungodly hour of nine o'clock in the morning. Normally, we attended two in a morning, skilfully arranged so that we did not have to get from Keble to Christ Church or from Worcester to Magdalen between the end of one and the beginning of the next. Then, the morning conscientiously completed, a solitary bread-and-cheese lunch in our rooms. Then – and this was the innovation in our lives – the whole afternoon was free, for games or walks or bookshops. Indeed, the whole of the rest of the day was free, unless there happened to be a five o'clock lecture or tutorial.

There were two temptations. One was to fill every afternoon with exercise, so that there was no chance of doing other sensible things. The other was to waste the whole of the time between lunch and Hall dinner doing nothing in particular. We gradually learnt that the crucial part of the day was between five o'clock and seven o'clock. A great deal of reading could be done then, especially of set books or straightforward narrative; and in later years I solemnly warned my pupils that their Class in the Schools would be determined by the amount of work they did in those hours.

But of course the real time for work was after Hall in the evenings. The practice was that we worked from eight until ten, knocked off for coffee in somebody's room and then either did or did not go on working after that. Usually we did, until any hour, enjoying above all the freedom to dispose of our time as we liked and not as any school timetable might require. The best essay I ever wrote was done right through the night, and I took it rather hard that I should be rebuked by the Dean for lying abed late as he met me making my heavy-eyed way across the Back Quad to a bath just before a ten o'clock tutorial.

Queen's in those days had a remarkable collection of dons. The Provost was John Richard Magrath, who had been Provost in my future father-in-law's undergraduate days and had retired from public life, though not from his office or his lodgings, shortly after that. When I had been there for three years and never set eyes on the Head of my College, I protested to a friendly don: 'I don't believe there is a Provost. He's been dead for years and the myth of his continued existence is kept alive by his housekeeper and the Pro-Provost, because if he did not exist their jobs would disappear.' 'Nonsense; of course he exists; I'll take you to tea at the Lodgings next Sunday.' He was as good as his word. And there was the Provost, clothed and in his right mind, just like his portrait in Hall, munching his own special kind of cake and unexpectedly clear about my identity and history.

The Pro-Provost was Edward Mewburn Walker, author of the definitive article on Greek History in the then current edition of the Encyclopaedia Britannica. He was almost totally blind: and we genuinely admired his recitation from memory of his part in Chapel services, including a long and complicated commemoration of our founder and benefactors. It was only later that I learnt that the same applied to his lectures on the Peloponnesian War. I had inherited my future father-in-law's notes of those same lectures as given some thirty years before, and after attending the first three I found that there was no need for me to go to any more, for they were indeed the same, *verbatim*.

The aforementioned Dean was John Bell, afterwards High Master of St Paul's. He was a tubby, boisterous man, with a heart as big as his waistline, and a voice which split the ear-drums in his idiosyncratic rendering of 'Alfonso Spagoni, the Toreador'. He was perhaps not at his best the morning after a meeting of the College dining club: what he did superbly was steer innocent Northerners through the academic and social complexities of Oxford College life.

But I suppose the most distinguished, certainly the most distinctive, of all the Fellows of the College was Thomas William Allen, the god. Tall, spare, handsome, straight as a ramrod, he clumped down The High to Queen's from his house in St Michael's Street, known and recognised by everybody. He had two mannerisms. He cleared his throat, with equal impressiveness, audibility and irrelevance, so that when he read as a lesson in Chapel the account of the delivery of the Ten Commandments to Moses, it began, 'And God spake all these words, saying: "I am – herh, herh – the Lord thy God." ' He also jerked his head violently upwards from right to left. An irreverent junior colleague once said, with deep affection, 'Our dear god has been trying to climb out of his collar for the past forty years: when will he learn that he can't?' He was, indeed, the god, the Olympian. Tutorials with him were terrifying. We paraded at twenty-minute intervals, at the most grotesque times of day. I shall never forget my first. At 4.20 on a Saturday afternoon I took in to him a Greek prose. I was gruffly bidden to sit by his side at his desk, where he sat with a rug across his knee by a window overlooking St Peter-in-the-East. I sat down and put my offering before him. He read it through slowly and in total silence, scratching out with a blue pencil one word in three, neck jumping out of collar. At the end he said, lengthily, 'Umm.' Then he went through it again, scratching out one word in three of what was left. Then I was dismissed to his bleak bedroom, to transcribe his own version, which, to judge from its battered yellow paper, he had written many years before. And that was that.

There were many other sides to him. He was an epicure, and on one night each week he had to dine with him an equally distinguished senior member of another college. To judge from the prior consultations with the College cook and the subsequent empties, their meetings were not confined to scholarly conversation. And as President of the College dining club he forbade potatoes. Further, he had a mischievous sense of humour. When I was unexpectedly invited to play hockey for the University against Cambridge I had to go to him for an *exeat* to permit me to be away from Oxford for the day and return after the locking of the front gate. I humbly submitted my request. 'Ho! The College is indeed (jerk, jerk) honoured. It is, I suppose, necessary (herh, herh) that you should go to London for this purpose?' I said that it was, since the match was at Beckenham. 'Very well, (herh, herh) go. Much as I deplore these (jerk, jerk) contests I have always taken the view that since they exist (herh, herh) it is desirable that we, and not (jerk, jerk) Cambridge, should win them. I trust we shall do so on this occasion.' Actually, we didn't.

There were others: B. H. Streeter, afterwards Provost, who said of himself, in the preface to a paper on *Alice in Wonderland* which he read to a College essay society, that in this life he enjoyed a canonry of Hereford Cathedral and in the next had been officially consigned to perdition for the expression of theological opinions not acceptable in the diocese of Zanzibar; G. B. Cronshaw, the bursar whose figure justified him in saying, when he was made Principal of St Edmund Hall, that he had been translated to the most capacious shelf in the University; C. H. Thompson, the mathematician, who arrived at High Table one night dressed in dinner jacket but without tie and, on being so informed, made his way out the length of Hall to riotous applause which was redoubled on his subsequent return with one; E. A. Berrisford, the Chaplain, who as President of the Oxford University Boat Club dropped himself from the crew ten days before the Boat Race because he thought he did not deserve his place; the modern linguist Wilfred House, a friendly and dapper military figure who was afterwards Master of Wellington; Godfrey Elton, a romantic hero who was said to have kept himself alive as a Turkish prisoner of war by eating his boots, and whose history lectures drew some of the biggest audiences in Oxford; A. H. Sayce, whom we hardly ever saw but recognised with awe as a world authority on Assyriology; Caballus Carter, the medical don, a Northcountryman of deep modesty and high distinction; – 'and others many', as our benefactors' prayer had it. These were all part of the background. The foreground was filled by those to whom we took weekly compositions and, later, weekly essays. They in themselves, Allen and Bell and Walker and Paton, were a pretty formidable lot.

But there was one other College figure, and he was unique, Sidney Steele, the Head Porter. Broadly built, his protuberance tightly encased in a double-breasted jacket, surmounted by a spotlessly clean stiff white collar and black tie decorated with pearl tie-pin; above that, a very clean-shaven face best described as florid and, inevitably, a bowler hat. He bustled; and he knew, unquestioned and unquestioning, that the College's name and fame, indeed its very existence, depended on him and him alone. With the senior dons he was on terms of dignified equality, based on reciprocal respect. The younger ones, especially if they were imports from other colleges like Balliol, he took in hand and educated in 'the way we do things at Queen's, sir'. To the rest of us he was a universal uncle-figure of boundless worldly wisdom and appropriate approachability, balancing tolerance and conscience with the shrewdness which can only come from a lifetime's experience of the growing up of young men. He was (predictably) a pillar of the Conservative Party in the ward where he lived: he was also (less predictably) a devout Catholic. I shall never part with the copy of *The Poets' Life of Christ* which Sidney gave me, absolutely out of the blue, on my twenty-first birthday.

We were proud of our College; and we had a good deal to be proud about – a perfect Hawksmoor building almost unchanged from the master's hand, a creditable record in Schools, a respectable place on the river, regular appearances in at least the semi-finals of most Cuppers, a well-known Musical Society, two flourishing Essay societies, and, above all, a sensible unsnobbish fraternal atmosphere which hindered nobody and helped a great many. We did not go in much for poets, or for the Union, or for the more 'social' of the University clubs. It all sounds frightfully old-fashioned and *mens sana in corpore sano*. All I can say is that fifty years ago one might have fared a good deal further and fared a good deal worse. Anyhow, I for one am very grateful for all that Queen's was and did.

Whether these sentiments were reciprocated I rather doubt. More than once I was officially rebuked for not doing enough work, and there was even a veiled threat of the removal of my scholarship. I suppose the truth was that so far as the Classics were concerned my heart was not really in it. Minute discussion of textual variants was not my cup of tea; and I somehow never had the proper passion for imitating the style of Demosthenes or Cicero. It might be more accurate, and more honest, to confess that Oxford had gone to my head. There were so many interesting things to do – a College team of some sort or other every afternoon, the Oxford Playhouse, Blackwell's, tennis-parties at Somerville, weekly addresses on 'God and Something-or-other' at St Mary's, and, above all, talk, talk, talk until the middle of the night – that set books and perverse unseens hardly seemed to be what I was there for. Nemesis was inevitable. There came the sickeningly black day when the telegram told me that I had got a Second in Mods. I shall never know what it cost my parents to put a brave face on it. To them, and, for that matter, to me, it was failure – made the harder to bear because my boyhood rival from the same school and the same College got a First. It was a fairly grim week.

It was the best thing that could have happened to me. If by some fluke I had got a First in Mods. I should inevitably have spent the rest of my Oxford years as I had spent the first five terms, and assumed that I should get away with it; and the result would have been a Third in Greats. As it was, the shock was salutary and the lesson was learnt. It was not so much a matter of doing fewer things. I did far more things, inside and outside Queen's, in my last two years than in my first two. It was rather a matter of focusing, of not frittering time away in a penumbra of vague and purposeless non-activity. In short, I was learning, the hard way, how to use time.

It is only fair to say that the subject matter of Greats was a great deal more congenial than that of Mods. had been. This, at last, was what Oxford was about. Freed from the schoolboyish business of artificial composition in dead languages, it was now necessary to write an essay out of one's own head and to defend it in face-to-face argument with a shrewd, learned and experienced tutor. Naturally, those early essays were almost totally derivative. But if I had to discuss what Thrasymachus said in the first book of *The Republic*, at any rate it was necessary to read what Plato said, and what Nettleship said about what Plato had said, and to come to some sort of decision about what Wolfenden was going to say. And if a bit of Sandy Lindsay's current lectures came in handy so much the better. My tutor was H. J. Paton, a soft-voiced Scot in the best Oxford Idealist tradition, an authority on moral philosophy in general and Kant in particular. He was an elegant figure, his dead-white face and immaculately white shirt set off by jet-black wavy hair and black suit. He lectured with forefingers stuck deep in top waistcoat pockets; and his dramatic sense inspired one day the curtain-line, as the clock above him struck one, '... and then there are those philosophers who hold the paradoxical view that grass is really green.' It was he who prescribed for me in the Long Vacation a course of reading in the Russian novelists – which, I may say, has never ended.

The Ancient History half of the course was much less attractive. I simply did not give a damn how many Athenian triremes were engaged in the battle of Arginusae (or was it Aegospotami?) but that was what E. M. Walker expected us to care deeply about. Nor did I care whether a particular letter of Cicero was written on the Thursday or the Friday of a given week; I thought I was doing pretty well if I got it in the right year. To be honest, I do not think we were very well taught. There is an old teaching tag about starting where the learner is. There was absolutely no sign of that; we had to start where Walker was, and then sink or swim. I sank. I am the only person I know who got a First in Greats without completing the compulsory questions in the Ancient History papers.

Then Paton went to California for a year and I was farmed out to T. D. Weldon at Magdalen. Weldon (inevitably, from a distinguished music-hall comedian of the time, 'Harry') was not an Establishment figure. He was talkative, cynical, blasphemous, libertarian; he was a Hegelian and a Wagnerite. I came to know him very well later on, as a colleague and as a regular visitor with our family on holidays, when we tried to repay something of the debt I owed to him. Those who never got past the defensive hard-boiled exterior did not know him. He was a desperately lonely man, and desperately afraid of being suspected of anything like softness or sentimentality in ordinary human relationships. He was also desperately afraid of women; one of the bravest things he ever did was to exchange a guest-to-hostess kiss with my wife. In fact he rejoiced in our children; the eldest was his godson, and eventually his pupil, a young man after his own heart.

But all that was years ahead. When I first went to a tutorial with him it was an electric shock, after the suavity of Paton. He was working very hard, so I frequently had to go with my essay at eight o'clock in the evening. The reading of the essay and the subsequent argument went on for anything up to a couple of hours at which point I was bidden to shed my gown and have a drink. Then came more talk, some of it to me rather wild, some deflating criticism of some of the more renowned Oxford philosophers, some records of Wagner, another drink – and I had to scuttle up The High to reach Queen's by midnight. These are, if you like, superficialities or irrelevancies. The essential fact, which I partially recognised, was that he was a first-class teacher; sometimes outrageous, sometimes on a hobby-horse, but always perfectly lucid and apparently just as excited as if he were exploring these mysteries himself for the first time. And he never condescended; what I said, however jejune or brash, was taken seriously. He demanded a vast amount of reading from one week to the next, sometimes with the suggestion, 'Well, read all that and then write an essay about anything in it that interests you.' And if that isn't good teaching I don't know what is.

So rushed on the weeks and the terms and the vacations. I was still as bored as ever by the triremes and the precise stations of each Roman legion along the Danube. I was more and more involved in things outside Queen's – playing hockey for the University, with the most engaging collection of people I have ever had to do with, getting involved in wholly decorous dances at women's colleges, being ingenuously serious-minded at Streeter's mixed reading-parties at Jordans, and generally unfolding. But the focus and centre of my Oxford life was Harry Weldon's room in Magdalen and the strenuous intellectual exercise that took place there once a week.

Came the spring and summer of 1928. There had, naturally, been some talk of what I was going to do afterwards. The obvious choice was teaching, obvious because all I had to show was a Second in Mods. and a hockey Blue, and that somehow did not seem to add up to the Civil Service. The University Appointments Committee showered me with flimsies about improbable jobs in improbable schools. I was seen by one or two headmasters, whose reaction was less than ecstatic. And then, late one night, came a quite different suggestion, and it came from Harry himself. Magdalen would have to have another philosophy don besides himself; the crowds of people wanting to do 'the new School', *alias* P.P.E., *alias* Modern Greats, were so enormous that on top of the standard Greats intake there were too many for one man to cope with. Before I could say anything came the body-blow: 'Of course, it isn't on unless you get a First.' I had attended, and it was a high compliment that I had been admitted to it, a small class or seminar jointly conducted by Professor J. A. Smith and Professor H. H. Joachim, and J. A., who as Waynflete Professor was a Fellow of Magdalen, had apparently given his patriarchal blessing to Weldon's wild idea. Indeed, J. A. himself asked me if I would like to be considered for a similar vacancy which was about to occur in another college. But always with this nightmarish condition, a First in the Schools. It is bad enough to face the Greats examiners anyway; but to face them with the knowledge that your whole future depends on their judgment of you is almost beyond human endurance. I hope I never have to live through such a ten days again: the panic as you sit down, the intolerable fluency of the pens of everybody else, the girl who faints, the post mortems, the increasing recklessness, the total absence of any of the questions you had so carefully prepared – and all in the knowledge of what depended on it.

Eventually it was all over, and there remained a few days of exhausted bliss before the end of term. Then the weeks of waiting until the *viva*. During this period of post-examination depression I still had the gall to decline, rashly, bravely, stupidly but I hope politely, an invitation to attend for interview at the 'other college' to which J. A. Smith had proposed me. It was Magdalen or nothing now. But the weeks of waiting had this inbuilt consolation. If your surname begins with 'W' you have to wait a long time before your turn for a *viva* comes. By way of compensation you have to wait a very short time after the *viva* before the results come. As I went in to mine the history examiners rose from their seats and silently stole away. When afterwards I charged one of them with thereby jeopardising the constitutionality of the proceedings he replied, 'My dear boy, it was perfectly obvious that there was no question we could ask you to which you would have known the answer. We thought it was kinder to leave you to the philosophers.' And to the philosophers I was left, for fifty mortal minutes, during which each of the three employed to the full his own personal weapons of mental torture. Released, I tottered to Harry's room for the pre-arranged drink and a blow-by-blow replay. I believe he was as worked up as I was. It was known that the class-list would be posted that same afternoon. Fortunately, the Examination Schools lie between Queen's and Magdalen; so when I had seen the list, having with proper superstition fixed my eyes first on the Second Class, I was able to manage the short journey to Magdalen, for the second time that day, to gasp to Harry, 'It's all right,' and then, inevitably, a drink. It had been a good omen that on the previous afternoon, playing for the Queen's College Servants C.C., quite illegally but under heavy pressure from my scout, I had made the highest score of my undistinguished cricket career.

The idea was that my name should be submitted to the President and Fellows of Magdalen in the autumn and that if I were elected I should start in at the beginning of the following academic year. That meant that in any case I had to find something to do for twelve months: 'Go away and play,' was the advice I was given. By great good fortune there was no problem. A few months earlier I had been attracted by the possibility of a year abroad. Whatever I was going to do after Schools there could be no harm in a year's break, and there might be a lot of good. So I had put in an application for a Henry P. Davison scholarship. There were three a year from Oxford (and three from Cambridge), one each to Harvard, Yale and Princeton. They had been established, and were financed, in memory of Henry P. Davison by his widow. He had been President of the American Red Cross during the First World War, a banker of international reputation, a convinced Anglophile and a trusted friend of American presidents and British governments. To perpetuate his name and work his widow founded what were in their modest way Rhodes Scholarships in reverse between these two English universities and the three American ones. I had applied, and I had been interviewed. I had no particular feelings as between the three American host institutions – I knew very little about them – but one or two Oxford friends recommended Princeton. Just before the traumatic experience in the Examination Schools the message came from the chairman of the interview board that I had been selected and would I please report at Princeton in September.

I was in no mood for retrospective introspection, and anyway there was never time for such luxuries. But I suppose that if I had been stopped in my tracks at this point and asked what I thought had happened to me over the past four years I should have had to make some reply. I had, I think, ceased to be callow without ceasing to be ingenuous; I had experienced some salutary failures, academic and social; I had had some successes, academic and athletic; I had made many friends, throughout the age-range from eighteen to eighty; I had gradually developed some sense of proportion; and I had not conspicuously or often made a fool of myself.

But especially, and perhaps rather naively, I had become infected with an enthusiasm for the subject we then called philosophy. In those days, at Oxford anyhow, that word meant something quite different from what it seems to mean today. We really were concerned about the questions which had been raised by Plato, Aristotle, Aquinas, Rousseau, Kant, Hegel and, for that matter, the three Greek tragedians. We really did bother our heads about God, freedom and immortality, about what constitutes a good man or a right act, about the nature of a universal, and about the content of a moral obligation. Perhaps we were the last dying embers of that tradition. But with people about like Collingwood, Joachim, Joseph, Lindsay, Paton, Ross, J. A. Smith, Weldon, it is not surprising that the shades of Bosanquet and Bradley were still influential. All that has changed long since. The questions that worried us are now held to be non-questions, or even nonsense-questions; and when I try nowadays to read articles in *Mind* and the other professional journals I soon find myself bogged down in square root signs, hairpins and epsilons the wrong way round. Befogged and obsolete as we doubtless were, we enjoyed it; and I am glad that I did Greats when I did.

But on that summer day I was not thinking these anachronistic thoughts. The bits of the jigsaw of my future were falling very happily into place. I was more than willing to go away and play for a year at Princeton and then come back to Magdalen. 'Going down' was therefore not a sadness, for I had the confident hope that I was coming back. I had, of course, no glimmering of a notion what Princeton was going to be like.

3

Princeton University, U S A

[1928]

I crossed the Atlantic by the cheapest possible means, a slow, small, two-class American Line ship with the romantic name of *Minnekahda*. I had never been out of England before, except on a one-day trip to Boulogne to visit the grave of the uncle who had died on Armistice Day. So I had no preconceptions about ocean travel and no standards of comparison. After the turmoil of packing, farewells and general uprooting, the eleven days at sea were a blissful holiday. I shared a two-berth cabin with an older man, a lecturer in economics whose brother, by the wildest chance, had worked in the County Hall at Wakefield. There was plenty of congenial company in the second class, and we had the run of the ship except for one promenade deck and the first-class dining-room. There seemed to be a good many elderly ladies travelling alone – I expect they were really in their fifties – and it was on this voyage that I quite unintentionally began my lifelong collection of elderly ladies. They seemed to want a young man to talk to, as a kind of substitute son or nephew; and I was available, with nothing else to do, no biting problems, and a ready willingness to absorb their experience and learn from them about living in the United States. I was as really green as Paton's philosophers' grass.

Out of the haze and daze of a September afternoon appeared the Statue of Liberty and the Manhattan skyline. I have always been thankful that my first view of New York was from sea-level. No number of subsequent arrivals by air add up to that first one, emotionally or aesthetically. The effect was not that of the Englishman's first sight of the White Cliffs of Dover on his return from foreign parts, or the ancient Greek seaman's first sight of the temple of Poseidon at Sunion on his return from the Euxine. They were returning: I was arriving. They were home after adventures: I was adventuring far from home, both literally and metaphorically.

Sea travellers in those days were not as comprehensively shepherded as air travellers are now; a degree of private enterprise and personal initiative was required of a young man from overseas arriving alone with a year's worth of luggage in the bustle of a New York quayside. I was rescued by the brother of an old friend of my ex-headmaster's wife. That was my first experience of something I was to come to know in all its fullness over the next nine months, the incredible personal friendliness and unaffected hospitality of the ordinary American family. These particular folk had never seen me in their lives; their connection with me was so tenuous as to be invisible. But they met me, steered me through the Customs, bore me off to their home up the river and insisted their house should be my base while I was in the United States. What is more, they meant what they said, literally, whole-heartedly and permanently, and they genuinely enjoyed this spontaneous open-handedness. So, as my experience widened and deepened, did I, immensely, though even so, I guess, never as much as they did, in their blessedly unconscious unselfishness. What they said was, 'No trouble at all': what they meant was that no trouble was too much for them to take.

The journey to Princeton was safely completed next day, without incident, except for two trivialities. I was panic-stricken when the conductor took my railway ticket from me. No Englishman surrenders his ticket except at the station of arrival, apart from the rare occasions when they are collected on approaching a terminus. But the slip to fit into the hat-band seemed to be acceptable to my fellow travellers, so I held my peace, though I did not then (and do not now) understand the inwardness of the operation. The other triviality gave me an encouraging first impression of American taxi-drivers. It was dark when *via* Princeton Junction I arrived at Princeton Station – since, I understand, abolished. I knew that my address was Pyne Hall, though I had, of course, no idea where that was. I asked the driver of the one available cab to take me there. He repeated the address and asked me if I was quite sure it was Pyne Hall I wanted. I said I was. He smiled, and then he drove me the fifty yards from the station to Pyne Hall. He did not, as he easily might have done with a green foreigner, drive me half way round the town and then back again.

41

Next day I had another remarkable example of trouble-taking. There was a note asking me to call on V. Lansing Collins, the Secretary to the University. For what I had imagined to be a formal visit to 'make my number' he had set aside two hours – and he the top administrator of the whole University right at the beginning of a new academic year. He firmly established himself as my guide and mentor: 'Come to me about anything, financial, academic, social or athletic.' More, he had already made a provisional plan for my academic work and lined up the relevant professors there and then. 'I want you to have enough to do to keep you busy, but not so much as to make you work too hard.' It was an essential part of the Davison Scholarship philosophy that we lived on the campus as undergraduates, not as postgraduates in the dignified seclusion of the Graduate College. But our academic work was *à la carte*, by personal arrangement with the individual professors concerned. Collins had booked me for one postgraduate course in philosophy, one in political theory, a fourth-year undergraduate course on Plato, and some elementary economics and German, neither of which I had ever done before. And that, with minor adjustments, was my diet for the session.

Later on he manfully came to my rescue in what might have been an embarrassing financial difficulty. I had had a cheque in advance to pay my passage across the Atlantic. I had not understood that this was the first instalment of the total emolument but had supposed that it was a separate payment to cover transportation. As the months went by it gradually became clear that this was a mis-understanding. So I had to come to me in the remainder of the year about one-fifth less than I had budgeted on. The only thing to do was to go and see Collins and explain. I did. He saw no great problem. He took me to see the President of the University, John Grier Hibben, and narrated the misunderstanding. After the gentlest possible interrogation the President said that he would be glad to provide a further cheque for the amount in question. Whether it came from some private Presidential aid-fund or from his own pocket I shall never know. But it was typical of the whole atmosphere.

Shortly after our arrival my Cambridge colleague and I were bidden to visit Mrs Davison, our benefactress, at her Park Avenue apartment. She received us as if we were doing honour to her by being there. Kate Trubee Davison was a remarkable woman, by any standards. She had the money to fulfil without problem or question her ancestral traditions of Southern hospitality; she lived in taken-for-granted elegance, in New York or on Long Island; and she was a matriarch. We were immediately absorbed into the family, as honorary younger sons or elder grandsons, with overflowing generosity and a not imperceptible note of command. 'Here is a key to this apartment. It is at your disposal whenever you come to New York. At week-ends you are very welcome to the house on Long Island if you have nowhere better to go. But remember, if ever I hear of you spending a night in a New York hotel you go back to England by the next boat.' In my assembly of elderly ladies she was unquestioned and unrivalled queen.

The house on Long Island, when later on we did go there, was the nearest thing I had ever encountered to a Stately Home. For that is what it was. The house itself was a mansion in the Georgian style. The grounds sloped down, in one direction, to Long Island Sound, with a sea-water bathing pool and the excitement of watching at fairly close quarters the America's Cup yacht race. The estate was what might modestly be called extensive. So much so that when-ever a member of the family married the matriarch built a house on it for him or her and each one of them was entirely private and secluded. Inside the house there was, of course, an English butler; and there were usually sixteen or twenty to Sunday lunch. The focus was the Trophy Room, its walls adorned with the heads of all kinds of beasts which Mr Davison had shot but also, significantly, with the diplomas of the many honorary degrees which had been conferred on him by universities round the world. That was the room where, somehow, his spirit seemed to linger; and it was certainly the room where his children talked about him most freely. None of this gave the slightest impression of ostentatious luxury: it was all assumed as normal. It was exactly the same thirty years later when my wife and I stayed with the same hostess in the same Long Island paradise. There was just one difference. Thirty years before I had had splendid fun and games with a three-year-old boy, throwing him in the air, rolling him over and over, and generally choking him with excited laughter. Thirty years later I did exactly the same with his three-year-old son. Spanning the generations, Kate Trubee Davison was totally unchanged.

Meanwhile, Pyne Hall was a dormitory (unlovely word) on the

corner of the campus most remote from the major University buildings. A small bed-sitting-room was a come-down from the Hawksmoor proportions of the Back Quad of Queen's; but it was perfectly
adequate except for late-night sessions of more than half a dozen.
And, as at Oxford, there were bachelor dons (sorry, faculty) scattered about the building whose rooms did provide more stretching-
space. From the start I had an almost incessant stream of callers,
inspired no doubt in part by sheer curiosity but also, as I soon learnt,
by genuine and friendly desire to help.

The first mystery into which we had to be initiated was 'The
Clubs'. Princeton prided itself on not having fraternities. It therefore
did not have fraternity-houses. Instead it had Clubs. You slept and
worked in your dormitory; after your first year, during which you
ate Commons in a vast dining-hall, you had your meals, newspapers,
gossip and billiards in your Club. They were handsome detached
buildings set down the two sides of a wide street where except on
very special occasions no female foot ever trod. A Club was a self-
perpetuating community of some sixty or seventy people. Elections
were held once a year, and pretty harrowing they must have been
for the luckless candidates, as they hawked themselves round in the
desperate hope that they would avoid the ultimate humiliation of
being elected nowhere and being condemned to a continuation of
Commons with all that that meant in social failure. There was, of
course, a pecking order, and some Clubs went for socialites, some
for footballers, some for sons of a generation ago's members; and it
was a terrible thing if a boy was rejected by the Club to which his
father had belonged.

My Cambridge colleague and I were spared these anxieties. We
were most generously invited to spend three weeks in each of four
Clubs, to see which we found the most congenial and then settle in
that one. The only embarrassment was in making the final choice,
lest we should seem to be unappreciative of the friendly welcome we
had enjoyed in the others. But it had to be done, and we eventually
plumped for Cap and Gown, as being not too 'social' and not too
hearty. We made many friends, had endless arguments about the
respective merits of different kinds of football, the impending Presidential election, patterns of education, the British and American
theatre and all such subjects as are proper for undergraduate
argumentation.

This was the autumn of 1928, which, you remember, came before 1929 and America's economic upheavals. The word 'euphoria' was not used as freely then as it is now; but that is what America was enjoying – or suffering from. Our young friends and their families spent money like water. Princeton had no rules about spending the night in residence; if you arranged your lectures shrewdly enough you could concentrate them on to three days in the week; and New York and Philadelphia were dangerously accessible. As our social life developed it became a serious problem to decide at which end of the week-end Wednesday came.

This is not to say that academic obligations were shirked or neglected. My postgraduate class on Kant was conducted by a professor better known in Oxford than he was in Princeton, where his modesty and abstention from University politics led to his being under-rated. He kept us hard at work on the text, emphasising what Kant actually said rather than what subsequent philosophers had interpreted him as saying; and that was very good for me. My political theory course was compensatingly comprehensive, and after six weeks I found myself reading a paper on two French writers I had never heard of before. Elementary German for the supposedly mature was taught on the splendid principle of 'picking it up as you go along', through the medium of short stories.

The undergraduate Plato course had lasting consequences. It was given by Paul Elmer More, an American scholar of great distinction both inside the academic world and outside it. A dozen of us sat at a table translating the *Gorgias* aloud sentence by sentence round the class. After four or five sessions he stopped me as I was leaving the room. 'This isn't very much in your line, is it?' I tried not to sound uppish as I confessed that I had in fact done exactly this at school five or six years before. 'Would you care to come to my graduate class in Aristotle?' Indeed, I would, gratefully. And I did, most profitably. Years later he visited us in Oxford and generously talked to my then pupils, to such effect that when I called in on the twenty-first birthday party of one of them I was greeted with shouts of, 'We don't want you, we want the American professor' – so he was fetched and duly fêted. On that same visit he asked if he might bring to lunch a young American poet whom I might care to meet; he was introduced as 'Tom Eliot'.

All through the Fall work and play went breathlessly on, day and night. An Oxford University debating team visited Princeton; so did the British Ambassador. The trans-Atlantic Zeppelin arrived. On the night of a total eclipse of the moon the ugliest building on the campus was mysteriously burnt down amid scenes of unbridled rejoicing. At a Sunday lunch in New York John D. Rockefeller himself incorporated me into his family to the extent of including me in his traditional weekly distribution of dimes to his children and grandchildren.

That really was quite an occasion. John D. Rockefeller III was a class-mate at Princeton, as unassuming and unpretentious a twenty-year-old as you could imagine. Quietly and diffidently, as if he were asking a favour, he wondered if the two Englishmen might possibly care to spend a week-end at the family apartment in New York. Again, as with Mrs Davison, there was no kind of ostentation. We were automatically absorbed into a normal family dinner on the Saturday, and shown the Sunday morning sights of New York. Sunday lunch was in a different key, because grandfather was going to be there. He was, indeed; but otherwise it was just a family Sunday lunch. Until it ended. Then we were paid the supreme compliment. His custom was that as the family moved out of the dining-room after lunch on Sunday he stood at the door, wizened and rather shrunken but absolutely all there, holding in his left hand a little leather bag. As each member of the family walked past him his right hand went into the bag and emerged with a dime, which was handed to the passing relative. That dime, believe it or not, was that person's spending money for the forthcoming week. Mine was a precious possession for many years until it was stolen.

Two minor problems of day-to-day living emerged. The first was the impossibility of getting a decent glass of beer to drink. In those Prohibition days it was, of course, easy enough to get liquor, if you could afford it and knew where to go. But the filthy concoctions that were available had no connection whatever with the half-pints of College-brewed beer we had taken for granted at Queen's; and the staple milk with every meal in the Club simply had the effect of lifting my weight to a point which it has never reached before or since. One lesson I did learn from experience of Prohibition legislation and the widespread flouting of it, and it has been very useful since, is that it is not only useless but positively damaging to any society to enact in it laws which do not command the respect and acceptance of the members of that society.

Another consequence of this legislation was a growing collection of speakeasy tickets. Each of our friends had his own favourite one in New York, and each was anxious to introduce us to his, as being by far the best. I carried them about with me for years in my wallet, together with a slip setting out my marks in Greats, until it was stolen from a changing-room while I was playing hockey at a well-known Army ground years later.

The second problem was the apparently trivial one of getting any exercise. All forms of games-playing seemed to be centred solely in the 'Varsity squad', the aspirants to places in the University teams. The Oxford pattern of inter-college games did not exist, and such inter-Club contests as did take place were informal pick-up affairs for half an hour after lunch. The only solution was squash; but neither then nor later did forty minutes inside an enclosed box strike me as an adequate substitute for an afternoon in the open air.

This winter provided many and varied new experiences. One was the first attempt at ski-ing, on, of all places, a hill in New Jersey. It was not humiliating. But I could not really trust the damaged knee; and that first ski-run has been my last.

I learnt also the difference, in the United States, between the North and the South. My first piece of evidence was a man in the Plato class. He was a very friendly fourth-year undergraduate from Atlanta, Georgia. But I simply could not understand a word he said. There seemed to be no consonants at all, he slid from one vowel to the next with no connecting noises. The interesting thing was that all the East Coast Ivy League types had no difficulty whatever in comprehending what to me was 'ah-oh-ee-wah'. It is a remarkable, and perhaps significant, fact that in an area as vast as the United States nobody seems to have any serious difficulty in understanding anybody else, however different their places of residence and their intonations, whereas in a country as small as England mutual comprehensibility between a Geordie and a Cornishman is just about nil.

Deeper than this, a short visit to North Carolina, in an automobile which blew its top every hundred miles, revealed the deep and enduring differences, not to say conflicts, between Confederates and Yankees. I wonder if those domestic wounds are still wholly healed.

Another sociological fact was revealed by the Yale–Princeton football match. My Oxford Davison colleague at Yale invited me to be his guest for that great day in the sporting calendar. (At that time Princeton and Harvard were for some silly reason not on footballing terms, so the Yale match was the peak of the season.) My major recollections are three. First, the hospitality of my host, who was subsequently a colleague at one of my English schools. Second, the glorious, and gloriously irrelevant, build-up of bands, with their marching and counter-marching before the game began. To an outsider's eye, this was much more fun than the game itself. American football, with its set plays and halts and measuring tapes, is a poor alternative to the flow of a good game of Rugby football. Third, the distressing spectacle of so many young people suffering from the effects of bootleg booze. When Oxford play Cambridge at Twickenham a good many young men, and older ones too, have a drink or three. But never since have I seen so many youngsters, especially girls, totally incapable as in the Yale Bowl that day. Subsequent, more academic, visits to New Haven have served to correct an unhappy initial impression.

My Cambridge colleague and I spent Christmas at Chevy Chase, just outside Washington, with yet another Princetonian family. The father was a retired admiral, who had been involved in naval aircraft in the First World War. The son, our Princeton friend, was studying to become an architect. Their house had none of the unspoken splendour of the Davison residences, but it was, so to speak, a very attractive Walton-on-Thames kind of family home, and there was a disciplined decorum which was almost English. There was deep snow, which mercifully made golf impossible and provided the perfect scenic background for a first visit to one of the most beautiful cities in the world. It is easy enough to say that like all 'new' capitals Washington is a city *manqué*. Doubtless it lacks the catholicity of life that is inherent in London or Paris; and it has, of course, its seamy and squalid side. But its spaciousness and the imaginative dignity of its proportions give to its public face a distinction of its own. Subsequent visits have done nothing to dim or diminish the first impression of outward serenity – not even the one my wife and I paid nearly forty years later for the funeral of our elder son who had died there.

In the Fall we had the excitements of a Presidential election – and if that description is not constitutionally correct it is what everybody called it. We had heard all the pre-election speeches on the radio, with Al Smith's celebrated Brown Derby thrown in; and we had sat up all night to listen as the results came through. We had, in a bewildered English way, not really been able to discover, either from public utterances or from our friends' private views, what distinguished Republicans from Democrats. Accustomed as we were to at least some degree of continuity and predictability in the policies of the major political parties at home, it seemed to us that in American politics one party came out at its Convention with a stitched-together programme of discrete items and the other had no option but to proclaim the opposite, without any discernible logic or identifiable policy on either side. However, this was not our business, except as yet another item in the fascinating kaleidoscope which was being presented to us.

Now all the hubbub was over and Mr Hoover was to take office as President of the United States. The elder Davison son was a member of the Government, and we in consequence were greatly privileged. We stood on a damp spring morning and watched with scores of thousands of others as Mr Hoover was sworn in as President. And we watched the incredible procession that made its way past him – uniforms of the Armed Forces from the Civil War to the First World War, State Governors with what seemed to be their private armies, the whole Diplomatic Corps suitably fortified by national dress – the lot, to the extent of more than two hours in pouring rain. And in the evening the Inaugural Ball. More people crowded into one room than anybody had ever seen anywhere before. Mr Hoover was not present, so the Vice-President, Mr Curtis, was host, and a very generous one too, to his stray British guests at least. It was engaging and instructive to see a man with obvious Indian blood in serene control of an international party of the highest possible protocolic significance.

About this time the admirable Collins wondered if I might not after all take a Master's degree. It would, if no more, be something to show for a year at Princeton. We went into it all at some length. I stood firm on the doctrine that a Davison scholar was expected to live as an undergraduate; deeply as I appreciated the generosity of various professors in permitting me to take part in their courses, graduate or undergraduate, I was sure that Mrs Davison (whose word was law) would not like to see her beneficiaries tied down to degree requirements. Eventually, after wholly amicable academic argument, we agreed that I should not offer myself for a Master's degree. There were in fact technical requirements which would, if they were to be conscientiously fulfilled, cramp my academically free-lancing style; and (privately) I could not see what a Princeton M.A. would add to a First in Greats. So I left Princeton without a degree – but with a great deal which was more valuable than two letters after my name.

In retrospect, I am bound to say, if it does not sound ungrateful and unappreciative, that I was not deeply impressed by the standards of undergraduate instruction at Princeton in those days. Graduate studies were an entirely different matter, whether conducted as private research in the Graduate College beyond the golf links or shared with the likes of me by courtesy of individual professors. The normal, and almost sole, vehicle of undergraduate instruction was the lecture. The audience might number twenty or sixty; and no doubt the lectures, as lectures, were good. But after the one-to-one contact of an Oxford tutorial system there seemed to be lacking a whole dimension, and that the most important. Sometimes questions were invited at the end of a lecture. But anybody who has ever done any teaching knows that the style and idiom of a question-and-answer session at the end of a lecture are wholly different from a face-to-face tutorial. The standards at Princeton were high: but for me, poised between having lately been a pupil and becoming shortly a tutor, they did not, to put it gently, set new goals.

Meanwhile, the major local event of the spring was dramatic, in the literal sense. An enterprising Anglophile Instructor (i.e. junior don) in the English Department thought it would be a good idea to put on a production of *Lady Windermere's Fan* for the edification of Princeton society. As a by now old friend he asked for my assistance in the general presentation 'to get the idiom right' and, in particular, as myself portraying Lord Windermere. I tried to explain that nobody could be less suited than I, from my background and upbringing, to fill the double glove he was fitting on to me. But to him an Englishman was an Englishman, and therefore an authority on all things English. Rehearsals were hilarious. The cast was recruited from the upper crust of Princeton society; but I was the ultimate arbiter of accent and mannerism in turn-of-the-century English aristocratic society. My chief personal embarrassment, when it came to it, was that because of the brevity of one interval I had to wear a boiled shirt under a blue suit throughout one act so that I might be ready in tails for the next. Eventually we presented ourselves to an audience which, bless its heart, was already so benevolently conditioned to what we were attempting to do that we could not have failed even if we had been worse than we were. Links of international friendship are forged by odd bits of machinery.

I spent Easter in Montreal, with a friend who was working on the *Montreal Star* and could therefore give me the necessary background for the understanding of that complicated and fascinating city. At one party the ultimate paradox was disclosed to me by a retired English major. 'You realise, of course, that it is the presence of the French in Canada that has kept Canada British. If it had not been for this indigestible linguistic and religious minority Canada would have been swallowed up by the Americans long ago.' I did not then, and I do not now, know whether he was right. But I saw what he meant, though perhaps his vision was too closely concentrated on Quebec to give proper attention to the Prairie Provinces or British Columbia. It is the sort of remark which, trotted out over the years in England, or even in Canada, establishes one as an expert.

On the train back to New York I was rather surprised to be thoroughly grilled by US Immigration officers. Where had I been? How long for? Where was I going to? How long for? Had I a job in the States to go to? By sheer chance I had in my pocket a letter addressed to me at Princeton; but it took many miles of railway journey to convince my interrogators that I was not using Canada as a back door into the heavily protected labour market of the United States.

Soon after Easter there was a letter from Weldon at Magdalen. It was essential that I should be in Oxford by June 27th, because on the morning of that day was the College Meeting at which I was to be elected to a Fellowship and it was necessary to be present in person. It also conveniently happened to be a degree-day, so I could be elected in the morning and take my degree in the afternoon. Everything was buttoned up and in order; all I had to do was be there.

That put a complete and final end to all plans for travelling across the continent or plunging into the deep South after the end of the Princeton term. Both possibilities had been exhaustively discussed with Princetonian friends, but both were now dismissed. It was in many ways a pity not to be able so to spend a few weeks while I was there, because heaven knew when I should be there again. But the Oxford commitment was inescapable; and steps must be taken at once to fulfil it.

There was another reason why I was not altogether sorry to be summoned back in this way. 'Mid all the pleasures and palaces of these nine months there had been one permanently hanging cloud, not obtrusive for all of every day but never entirely absent from the sky. Before I left home I had come to an understanding with the girl I was going to marry. We were not officially or formally engaged. In those days, in our walk of life at any rate, people did not get engaged until there was some fairly visible prospect of the man's being able to support a wife; and I had not yet started earning. Neither of us had any doubt about the ultimate outcome. But nine months was a long time to be separated from each other. We corresponded, frequently and fervently. But there were no air mails then; and it was of the first importance to catch the *Aquitania* or the *Majestic* and not to get our letters stuck on a slow boat or held up by fog. Continuity of communication was not easy in such circumstances, and I should be very glad to see her again.

So I booked myself on the *Laconia* for the beginning of June, as a compromise between excessive cost and intolerable slowness, and could hardly wait. There was a genuinely regretful round of farewell visits, to friends in Philadelphia, Washington, New York, and, especially, to the incomparable Mrs Davison. She had made it all possible, and when she asked me what I thought I had learnt I could make no coherent reply. I could not know then how invaluable this experience was to turn out to be, with Rhodes scholars in the coming Oxford years, with American universities in the years further ahead, with colleagues on the Fulbright Commission in London, with streams of American visitors to the British Museum and with individual ambassadors of the United States in Grosvenor Square and Regent's Park. There are still occasions when it seems fitting that I should, with proper pride, wear my Princeton tie.

4

Magdalen College, Oxford
[1929]

There was, and I hope there still is, an engaging ceremony at Magdalen for the admission of a new Fellow. The neophyte was summoned to the New Room, where the President and Fellows were assembled. He knelt on a velvet cushion at the feet of the President. The President, in Latin, required him to give his oath to observe the statutes and by-laws of the College. The expected and proper answer was '*Do fidem*'. The President then formally admitted him, raised him to his feet and shook his hand with the words, 'I wish you joy'. The fledgling then walked round the room, to be greeted by each of the Fellows in order of seniority with those same words. Each had his own way of pronouncing them, formal, warm, facetious or (from Weldon) sardonic.

For his first year he was technically a Probationer Fellow, though that apparently undignified status made no difference to his workload or his salary. During that time he attended College Meetings but did not vote. He was not regarded as competent to carry round the dessert in Senior Common Room after dinner; that was the heavy responsibility of the two junior Actual Fellows present. After a year as a chrysalis, and if he had not blotted his copybook, he became Actual, *verus*. He was elected for five years and then came up for re-election by the President and Fellows. Re-election was by no means automatic. During my five years there two quite senior Fellows were not re-elected by their colleagues, simply because they were thought not to be doing their jobs properly. In modern days of 'staff rights' and assumptions about security of tenure it may seem either shocking or surprisingly rigorous that in one of those battlemented bastions of privilege, an Oxford college of forty-five years ago, you had to justify yourself to your colleagues every five years if you were to survive.

Of those who had wished me joy two, Weldon and J. A. Smith, I already knew well; but most of the rest were as new to me as I to them – terrifyingly new, some of them. As an undergraduate I had found the Queen's dons a remarkable lot: now, as the most junior don in Magdalen, I found my colleagues far more remarkable. It was my great good fortune to be admitted to that company while some very potent, grave and reverend seniors were still there, and I learnt almost as much from them as I did from my pupils.

We who lived in College breakfasted in Senior Common Room, at a vast round table, at any time from eight o'clock onwards. This custom had its dangers. The oldest were the first to arrive; and not all of them had learnt, in their long lives, that the breakfast-table is no place for conversation. There were newspapers, and the more civilised of us took proper refuge behind them. But that did not provide complete escape from booming reminiscence or vituperative University politics. There was a compensating convention that nobody asked anybody to pass anything; you just reached for your marmalade or your cherry jam. And with a little experience you learnt not to arrive until X, Y and Z could safely be expected to have finished and gone to the Smoking Room next door – or to the other adjacent place. Lunch also was a Common Room affair, enlivened by other people's guests and earned after a morning's work. Before dinner in Hall we assembled in Senior Common Room and then processed, in order of seniority, along the Cloisters, up the stone stairway and the length of Hall to High Table. Here again seniority was punctiliously observed, with the President in the middle of the long side of the table, the senior Fellow present on his right, the next on his left and so on alternately down the line and round the other sides of the table. This arrangement meant that on a full evening the most junior Fellows found themselves opposite to the most senior ones, and the disadvantage of having one's back to the body of the Hall was more than outweighed by the conversation of these heroes and their guests.

That conversation was not always solemn. One evening the first strawberries of summer appeared. Cowley, Bodley's Librarian, a rubicund *bon viveur*, helped himself to a shovelful of them, a pound of sugar and a pint of cream. Sitting next to him was Brightman, a liturgiologist so learned that he was alleged to be capable of saying his prayers in every language of Europe and Asia. But he was dyspeptic: he turned on Cowley a baleful pale blue eye, put his little fists on the table, and said, 'Cowley, you are a lascivious old man.' Brightman was also the hero of a breakfast-table conversation with J. A. Smith. J. A. came booming in, protesting that he had just received a letter addressed to 'J. A. Smith Esq.', whereas, he thunderously maintained, it ought to have been addressed to 'Professor J. A. Smith'. 'My dear J.A., have you not yet learnt,' asked Brightman, more in sorrow than in anger, 'that "Professor" is not a title, it's a status – unless, of course, you are a conjuror?'

C. T. Onions, the encyclopedic editor of the Oxford Dictionary, tested me on the dialects of the West Riding of Yorkshire; and whenever he and I wanted to have a private conversation in public we dropped into a language which was incomprehensible to anybody but our two selves. Sherrington, the greatest physiologist of the day, confessed, with his shy sideways smile, that he had once, as C. S. Sherrington, published a slim volume of verses; one reviewer had said that they were less intelligible than Sir Charles' *Integrative Action of the Nervous System*, another that Miss Sherrington would improve with experience. Godfrey Driver, a non-athlete who walked immense distances with immense strides, maintained that the only exercise he ever took was following to their graves the coffins of people he knew who had played games.

The Senior Fellow was Paul Victor Mendelssohn Benecke, who since his schooldays had spent his whole life in the College, as a Scholar, called at Magdalen a Demy because in earlier days his emolument was half that of a Fellow, and then as a Fellow. In his youth he had been a prodigious pianist; but when I first knew him he had not touched a piano for twenty years, because he could no longer play as well as he used to. He was a man of totally upright and blameless life. And there therefore gathered round him totally unfounded legends of shocking depravity. Why had he been found unconscious and blood-stained at the foot of the staircase leading to the private apartments of the Principal of a ladies' college? How had a visiting foreign professor come to fall off Benecke's window-sill into the deer park below? Why, after forty years' experience of the precise location of the decanters in the Smoking Room, had he poured for an unwelcome guest alternate tumblers of brandy and whisky? It was Benecke who asked me, on my first evening as a Fellow of the College, if I was aware that I had already forfeited my Fellowship. Dumbfounded and twittering I asked how or why. With the gravest of faces he said it was because I had that afternoon committed an academic act from another college. I stammeringly explained that I had thought it necessary to be presented for my degree from Queen's because it would have been arrogantly presumptuous to anticipate my election at Magdalen that morning. I was assured, with a bleak smile, that he would not himself call attention to my misbehaviour if nobody else did.

There was A. L. Dixon, a Professor of Mathematics who perhaps took more interest in his flute-playing than in his formulae; and C. H. Turner the theologian, who rocked a College Meeting by declaring that 'if the College wants to do that sort of thing the College can't do that sort of thing in that sort of way.'

In the middle band of seniority, between the elders and myself, there were those whose lives had been sharply interrupted by the First World War fifteen years earlier. Weldon was one of those who had gone straight from school into the Army, and I always suspected that the slight deafness which led him to play Wagner so loud had been caused by the guns he had served. C. S. Lewis belonged to the same generation, one of the most stimulating talkers of the day but not easy to get to know. To all outward appearance he might have been a farmer, with his big red face and booming voice. Nobody would have suspected that behind this jolly bucolic outside there was a sophisticated theologian and a sensitive writer of imaginative children's stories. Some of us, academic snobs that we were, thought it odd and wasteful that he should be teaching, of all things, English literature when he clearly had the intellect to be teaching philosophy. To keep his hand in, as he modestly put it, he would be grateful if I would allow him to take some of my pupils for moral philosophy while I took some of his in the elements of metaphysics and logic. I was delighted to expose mine to his acute and scintillating mind, and I suspect that they got by far the better of the exchange.

Michael Parker, the historian of the Roman Army, was as Senior Dean responsible for undergraduate discipline. His techniques were very different from those to which I had been accustomed under the boisterous regime of John Bell at Queen's. He prided himself on knowing the family backgrounds, idiosyncrasies and even personal secrets of each member of his flock; so that if disciplinary action had to be taken it was carefully designed to make the punishment fit the criminal rather than the crime. He had no use for the view that there was a fixed tariff for breaking windows or climbing into college or having young ladies in rooms outside the permitted hours. Some people thought some of his decisions rather unaccountable or even capricious. But there was in fact very little crime, of even the mildest kind – partly because the young very considerately did not want to give him the sleepless nights they knew to be involved in his painstakingly working out the penalty appropriate to each particular offender.

Malcolm MacKeith left us soon to be Dean of the British Postgraduate Medical School at Hammersmith. Not the least remarkable was Adam Fox, who arrived shortly before I did but by a very different route. He was then in his middle forties; he had been Warden of Radley and a schoolmaster in South Africa. He came to Magdalen as Dean of Divinity, an office which enabled him to exercise such pastoral care in the College as might be congenial both to him and to undergraduates, and also to teach in a not very demanding way such subjects as might interest him. He was a joy to have around, with a gentle simplicity of mind and spirit, a talent for writing English verse and a turn of phrase which was sometimes straight eighteenth-century. One of the bravest things I ever did was to teach him to drive a car: he had an unnerving faith in the efficacy of prayer.

There were others who were nearer to my own age. John Christie had just come, after some years of teaching Classics at Rugby, to deal with the Greek and Latin of Honour Mods. He brought with him some salutary schoolmastering practices, including an Unseens examination on Saturday mornings at nine o'clock, which were not always popular with young gentlemen who supposed that they had now put away childish things. His own self-discipline, in such matters as physical exercise and cold baths, put the rest of us to shame. This is not to suggest that he was a joyless figure – far from it. He enjoyed a ribald joke as much as anybody, provided that it was funny as well as rude. He left us to become Headmaster of Repton; and it was one of the uncovenanted benefits of my years at Uppingham later on that he and I visited each other often when our two schools confronted each other at cricket or hockey. We found as headmasters that we had a good deal in common, and I learnt much from him about the management of colleagues and parents. It was typical of him that after two distinguished headmasterships and the headship of an Oxford college he went back, in retirement, to part-time teaching at Westminster.

There was Bruce McFarlane, already in his thirties a distinguished medievalist, whose cat bore the same name as Dr Johnson's; Pat Johnson, a physicist Rowing Blue whom the Second World War removed to the *arcana* of Defence administration; Bill Mackenzie, afterwards a professor at Manchester and Glasgow; and others many, up to a total of thirty-five – a big Senior Common Room for those days.

Over this galaxy presided George Gordon, formerly Professor of English at Leeds and then at Oxford. He would never have claimed to be a 'figure', and he was not one of those Presidents around whom mythologies collect. But by sheer friendliness, good temper and native shrewdness he kept his team of wayward individualists together, so that we were not, as some other colleges were, rent by schism or plagued by personal bitternesses. There was plenty of liveliness at College Meetings, and a fair amount of hard hitting; but none of it was below the belt, and nobody was not on speaking terms with anybody else. We were an egalitarian élite, based on reciprocal respect and, yes, affection.

Not everybody had the same sort of job. Professors professed, researchers researched, bursars looked after the money and the administration. Those of us who were labelled 'Official Fellow and Tutor' staunchly held that we did the real work, teaching and lecturing to the young. I reckoned to do a twenty hours a week teaching programme, on a one-to-one or two-to-one basis; and when Weldon went off on a Rhodes Travelling Fellowship and left me his pupils as well as my own it went up well beyond that. There can be all sorts of argument about the Oxford teaching pattern of those days – its ludicrous extravagance in manpower, its fundamental folly in applying to the mediocre ordinary chap methods which could at best be justified only for the first-class scholar, the excessive influence of one tutor on his flock, and so on. I can only say, from experience at both ends of the relationship, that although it may be far from perfect, human beings being human, I do not know a more fruitful or effective way of instructing the intelligent young. The number of my pupils, over five years, who got Thirds in the Schools was (just) higher than the number who got Firsts. But I do not believe that my time was wasted on the Thirds; and I do believe that I 'did more' for some of them than for some of the Firsts, who would probably have managed perfectly well without me anyway. There are, or at least there were in those days, a good many young men (and women) for whom their Class in the Schools was not the be-all and end-all, but who nevertheless profited, in ways I should be hard put to it to define, from having to defend their weekly essays and stand up to an hour's academic discussion with somebody who was not much older than they were but who was supposed to know more about the particular topic of discussion than they did. It has by now become standard practice that any government which is formed in this country has to include a former pupil of mine who got a Third in Modern Greats.

I never saw myself as a profound or original philosopher. I liked teaching, and I particularly enjoyed watching and guiding the first steps which the young took in this fresh field after their emancipation from subjects they had studied at school. I lectured on a general introduction to philosophy each summer term, and then, to give myself the discipline of expounding a particular text, on Aristotle's *Ethics*. I did not profess an intimate knowledge of all the post-Kantians and I gladly sent my pupils to the experts on specialist topics, taking in return their pupils for moral philosophy or the Greek texts. Fortunately, Weldon was especially interested in the Germans and in political philosophy, so we easily established a fair division of labour between us; and I continued to learn from him and J. A. Smith.

It was hard work, because, as every teacher knows, the time spent in what is nowadays frighteningly called 'person-to-person contact' is only the tip of the iceberg. Journals have to be read, professional society meetings attended, and lectures prepared; and we had College Meetings and committees as well. But it was not all work. In the summer a splendid College cricket club played round the adjacent villages. And squash kept in due perspective epic bowls battles on the lawn in Cloisters after the Senior Common Room port. There was an entertaining club which had out a standing challenge to play anybody at any game, on the understanding that the club's team would be composed of people whose game that was not. So when we played the Oxford City Police at soccer it was with a team of rugger players.

Hockey took an increasing amount of my time. Almost every week-end between Christmas and Easter I was involved in a match of some kind, at county or divisional or international level, and the travelling involved added to the complications of a crowded programme of lectures and tutorials. Once I had to spend ten days in bed, mercifully not in term-time, as the result of being hit on precisely the same spot on the side of the head twice in one game. On another occasion, playing against Scotland, I was hit on the point of the jaw in the last minute of the game by something I never saw. To revive me the hospitable Scots filled me with neat whisky, and I might easily have died if I had not been gloriously sick two hours later. Years afterwards I met again the man who had made the shot; he said he had belted it as hard as he could from five yards' range and when I went down he thought he had killed me.

Another time we were nearly beaten by Germany in Hamburg. The crowd resembled an English Cup Final gathering rather than the decorous sprinkling of spectators we were used to at home. They became almost frenzied with unconcealed partisanship. If we had won we might easily have been lynched for winning and the German team for losing: an uncontrived draw saved us all. So there was a fair amount of fun and games and relaxation as well as an honest term's work.

Pupils added to the gaiety. One, a distinguished aristocrat from Siam, who coxed the University VIII, had the habit, on the evenings of twenty-first birthdays or other celebrations, of stripping down to a scarlet bathing-dress and climbing about the College intoning, 'Cogito, ergo sum.' His own farewell party was notable for the presence of a boatload of American lovelies who had come to Europe for the wedding of another pupil, and for a brilliant farewell speech in verse composed and recited by the stroke of the University boat. Another had a cricket ground in the ancestral park and his country-house cricket-week guests were called in the morning with the choice of tea, Eno's or lager. A third drove a lethal Italian car to the great danger of everybody, especially his passengers, and when rebuked by other road-users waved his arms and cried, 'Non capisco.' The less gilded, hard-working scholars who desperately wanted Firsts, had regrettably little time for frivolities, but they got their

Firsts and became professors, parsons, schoolmasters or civil servants. Every evening some of the young would come and drink beer in my rooms – not the same ones always, and sometimes they brought friends from other colleges. Everything under the sun was discussed, from Aristotle to their girl-friends, from possible jobs to our prospects against Cambridge. It was a good life, against the backcloth of Magdalen Tower, Cloisters, New Buildings, Addison's Walk and the fritillaries in the Meadow.

After three years of this, on September 10th 1932, Eileen and I were married. It had been a foregone conclusion for a long time; the only question had been when it should happen – and that meant when we could afford it. My total salary from the College was six hundred pounds a year; and although I had not managed to save much we thought we could live on that. She had been a fairly frequent visitor to Magdalen from her art school life in London; she had been hospitably and generously received by the President and his family; and she had met a good many of my young men. So there was no surprise or shock about it; and the goodly company assembled at St John's, Wakefield, on the fatal day included as ushers an elegant selection of Magdalen undergraduates.

The reception was held at the home of the bride's parents, which I now entered less diffidently than I had done when I first knew it as the Headmaster's house. The two fathers and the bridegroom made the appropriate speeches; the two mothers made the necessary introductions; my uncles and aunts, in their Sunday best and rather overawed, mixed with the cream of Wakefield society; the bride's attendants wore elegant period costumes of her own designing; and the happy pair eventually left for an undisclosed destination.

We were lucky enough to find the perfect house in Holywell, opposite New College. It belonged to Merton College, who turned out to be generous and understanding landlords. It was one room wide, two rooms deep and three storeys high, so it was not too big to furnish out of wedding presents but certainly big enough for two people. Actually, it held three, because my six hundred pounds allowed us, in those high and far-off times, to have a living-in maid. She was 'Army Amy', a Salvation Army lass from the Channel Islands, of about our own age, 'cradled,' as she said, 'in the Army,' in which both her parents had been active. She was quick, nimble, volatile, energetic and totally devoted. Her only stipulation, in coming to us, was that she should have three evenings in the week free for the Army; and on these evenings, complete in uniform and bonnet, she went out to do battle for the souls of Oxford. One fifth of November I warned her that her bonnet might not survive the general boisterousness of that particular date; but she would not compromise. When she came in she had no bonnet, but with her usual good humour she hoped that as a trophy it might sometimes remind its captors of their sins.

Moving out of College inevitably changed the pattern of my daily life, but much less than if we had gone to the wilds of North Oxford or Headington. We were only two minutes' walk from the Long-wall Gate of Magdalen, and my teaching day was unaltered. Nor did the young cease to come and drink beer; indeed, the presence of a presentable young wife was perhaps an added attraction. They came either by the front door or by the less conventional entrance of the first-floor window, which was the more accessible because the ground floor was two steps down from street-level. This was the normal approach of a distinguished South African Test Match cricketer and Rugger Blue who was not technically a pupil of mine but as an enthusiastic village-cricketer a very welcome beer-pal; we never knew when his rather monkey-ish face might appear at the window and mouth a request for admission and refreshment. We dined out in the hospitable Oxford of those days, either in bridal white with the more formal elders or in anything-or-nothing with the young. We had distinguished neighbours, the Vicar of St Mary's, the Mallams, Michael Holroyd, J. Z. Young and his wife next door. The little garden at the back was remarkably fertile, because, as we were told, we were just outside the City wall and all the corpses had been thrown over there at the time of the Great Plague. Magdalen was as lovely as ever, and all went merry as a marriage bell.

But for some reason or other I began to feel unsettled. I am not quite sure why. For one thing, I was pretty clear that I was not likely to produce any epoch-making original philosophical thoughts. My first book had been published in 1932 and reasonably well reviewed, even by the redoubtable Dr C. E. M. Joad, who said that although he disagreed with every one of my personal conclusions he found it 'of its kind and for its purpose first-rate'. But it was, and was intended as no more than, a general introduction to philosophy for the use of people just beginning Greats or Modern Greats. I did not see myself concentrating for a lifetime on the problems of perception or the analysis of a sentence. Secondly, if I was going to be mainly a teaching Fellow all my life I had one or two living warnings among my colleagues, men in their fifties still trying to keep up with the young, whether on the cricket field or in the pub, and sometimes presenting a not very edifying spectacle while they were at it. Thirdly, there may have been an element of North-country Puritanism coming out. It was all too enjoyable. In those early 1930s Oxford in general and Magdalen in particular were just too good to be healthy. If ever there was a Lotus-land this was it; and although I was not (and am not) conscious of a deliberate rejection of these seductions – indeed, I totally immersed myself in them – I should not be surprised if without my knowing it there was a Methodist worm gnawing somewhere inside.

But what else was there for me to do? I was by now too old for the Civil Service competition, and also by now more accustomed to setting and marking examinations than to sitting them myself. Nor did I quite fancy schoolmastering. In an academically snobbish way I was reluctant to step down from teaching philosophy at the best college in the best university in the world to teaching Latin and Greek to the Lower Sixth at some bleak barrack in the Midlands. Tentatively and timidly I talked things over, in ghastly secrecy, with two or three friends, including, of course, George Gordon, conscious that those who had helped me so generously to my present job might well feel that I was an ungrateful and ungracious churl.

Then somebody suggested not just schoolmastering but head-mastering. I think it must have been J. C. Masterman. J.C. was an extraordinary man. He had got an Athletics Blue before the First World War. He was a civilian internee throughout it, having been caught at Freiburg doing what I had done at Princeton, putting in a year between taking Schools and becoming a don. He had come back to Christ Church, played international lawn tennis and hockey, and operated as a Harlequin cricketer, a plus handicap golfer, and one of the dozen best squash players in England. During which, as George Robey used to say, he was the model History tutor and confidant. I had first met him on the hockey field, when his career was gradually ending and mine just beginning, and he took me under his wing, in that context and many others. On three important occasions in my life I went to him for dispassionate advice: I did not always take it, but that did not prevent me from going to him again or him from giving it again.

There had always been a trickle of dons from Oxford and Cambridge colleges to the headmasterships of public schools. John Bell, one of my tutors at Queen's, had lately gone to St Paul's. But these were usually men of middle age, with an established record behind them, either in scholarship or in administration. I had neither. But my advisers reckoned that there was nothing to be lost by having a bash; at the least, one would get the feel of the market. What is more, being practised men of affairs, they encouraged me to start high up in the league-table, on the shrewd ground that if I aimed high and did not succeed I could always, if I so wished, lower my sights, while if I started more humbly and failed there was nowhere to lower them to.

It happened that at that time there were two public school headmasterships about to fall vacant. I put in applications for both. The Chairman of the Governors of one of them wrote to George Gordon sternly enquiring on what grounds he or I supposed that I had any right to presume to begin at the top of a new profession, and recommending, in effect, a little more humility.

By the Governors of the other, Uppingham, I was summoned for interview. I suppose I went rather light-headedly, knowing that there was really nothing to lose, and not having taken in Weldon's dry comment, 'Be careful about going in for a job, there's always the risk that you might get it.' There were four of us, one already a headmaster and the others established senior housemasters at well-known schools. The Chairman was Claude Blagden, Bishop of Peterborough, himself formerly a don at Christ Church; and he was surrounded by a formidable company of Old Uppinghamians, industrialists, ex-schoolmasters, soldiers and clergy. Nothing could have been more courteous than their conversation with me. But I still could not quite believe that it was happening in the real world. I had, naturally, to disclaim any special knowledge of public schools, except in the persons of my Magdalen pupils; no, I had no particular views about compulsory membership of the OTC; yes, I had what I hoped was a healthy but not disproportionate interest in games; certainly, I should enjoy teaching the Classical Sixth – and other

The author aged four, 1910

Mrs Spilsbury
with her two elder
daughters, my wife,
Eileen (*right*) and
Clytie, 1912

Kate Trubee Davison, 1928

10 September 1932. The dresses were designed by the bride

forms too, right down the school, if time would permit. I volunteered one opinion. If they should by any chance consider appointing me, I would suggest, if I might, that it should be for a fixed term, perhaps ten years. I heard one of the old gentlemen say behind his hand to his neighbour, 'What he's after is security of tenure.' 'On the contrary,' I contradicted, 'I am now twenty-seven. If you were to appoint me, on the strength, presumably, of qualities which you think I may now possess, it seems to me quite likely that after ten years or so I shall not still possess them. I may by then have others; but at that point I think, if I may say so, that you ought to be free to make a change without any feeling of hardship or ill-will.'

The half-hour the four of us spent waiting together was not the happiest time of my life. It ended by my being invited to return to the Board Room and invited further to become Headmaster of Uppingham at the beginning of the Summer Term of 1934. I had just time to send a telegram to a waiting wife before catching the train to Oxford and an evening of rather stunned celebration with the good friends who had taken the astonishing risk of sponsoring this impertinent exploit.

5
Uppingham School
[1934]

The first night I ever spent in a boarding school was our first night in the School House at Uppingham. We moved in half-way through the Easter holidays. On the basis of this experience I have always maintained that this is a good time to start a new job in a school or a university. The momentum of the school year takes you through to the end of the Summer Term and then there are the summer holidays to enable you to take breath and think, so that you are ready to begin to earn your keep at the beginning of the September term; whereas if you start in September the chances are that you are pretty well a passenger for the whole of your first academic year.

There had been a good deal to do. The furniture of our tiny house in Holywell was wholly inadequate for an official residence – the first of many 'tied cottages' we were to inhabit. So with the help of a timely loan from the former boy-preacher uncle we had spent a fair amount of time and money equipping ourselves. We were lucky that it came just when it did; the early 1930s were, in retrospect at any rate, a remarkably favourable time for setting up house on the scale which was required of us. We were lucky too in acquiring all the handsome Victorian glass which had belonged to Edward Thring, my predecessor-but-three and the real founder of Uppingham – the School House seemed to be its rightful home.

There was also a considerable psychological adjustment to be made. I was no longer a young and carefree don living in Lotusland. I was 'The Head Man' or *tout court* 'The Man'. There were at least four housemasters old enough to be my father, and of a staff of thirty there were two who were younger than I was. My predecessor had been there for eighteen years, and the school was shaped in his autocratic mould. Discipline was firm, not to say rigid;

the school was better known for its invincibility at Rugby football than for intellectual achievement; and there had been only three headmasters between the great Edward Thring and me; three members of my governing body had been boys at the school in Thring's time.

Nothing could have been more friendly than our welcome. I never really discovered, all the time I was there, what these splendid colleagues, senior and more junior, had really thought when they had heard of my appointment. But however much of a shock it was they never let it show. They took me by the hand and led me through the minefield. Most particularly there was a long lean cadaverous man, just reaching retiring age, whom I inherited as Senior Master. He was universally known as Billy S., being one of three members of the staff with the surname of Saunders. He spent hours with me before my first term began, his wrinkled face creasing into knowing smiles, breaking into Latin or Greek when he wanted to impart secrets, even suggesting once that we should 'continue this conversation in the garden – you will learn that confidences are better exchanged in the open air where nobody can possibly overhear.' I treated him as I had treated my Oxford tutors: and perhaps he enjoyed having an ignorant innocent like me as a *tabula rasa*. If the school's transition from one headmaster, whom he had served with utter loyalty, to another, whom he might so easily have rejected, went off without disaster it was very largely due to the magnanimity of Billy S.

There was another, more domestic, dimension to which we had to grow. Instead of Army Amy we now had a domestic staff of butler, cook, housemaids, parlourmaids and gardeners, as well as a matron and the necessary dormitory maids for the boys' side. Here again we were most delicately steered. But it was not altogether easy for a twenty-six-year-old wife (and pregnant at that) to cope with all the daily details of a household of fifty boys as well as our private selves, even though she had been brought up as a headmaster's daughter. Like Billy S. in the school context the domestic staff combined in a remarkable way the respectful with the protective.

Then there was the surrounding population. This fell into two quite separate categories, the County and the Town. Uppingham is deep in the heart of England, where the north-south road from Nottingham to Kettering crosses at right angles the east-west road from Peterborough to Leicester, and the nearest of those towns is nearly twenty miles away. The ridges of the red earth of Rutland, the valley of the Welland and the north-east spur of what further down are the Cotswolds make its physiognomy. There are wide skies, fresh winds ('straight from the Ural Mountains' they used to say in winter), and not an industrial sign in sight until Corby began to show itself on the south-eastern skyline. It was Cottesmore country; and we had to make a considerable social adjustment to cope with all that that meant. One member of the staff, who claimed to have been born on a horse, had to have his teaching timetable so arranged as to leave him free from the middle of the morning on Tuesdays and Saturdays.

The Town was much nearer to our business and bosoms. Uppingham always liked to claim that it was one of the two towns in Rutland; but in fact it was simply a biggish village. And it was wholly dominated by the School, which in one way or another provided the livings of the great majority of the inhabitants. They worked in the boarding houses or maintained the buildings or kept the shops which the boys used. There was a published list of the shops which were 'In Bounds', and to be removed from that list meant economic ruin: the story went that one shopkeeper had been so punished for the heinous crime of acting as post office between some wicked boys and some of the lasses of the village. So the Headmaster had considerable power in the life of the Town. There was no squire, as there was in most of the surrounding villages; and he in many ways had to fill that gap; and the Rector, leading his flock, beamed on the new young couple suddenly planted in the School House.

The beginning of term loomed. Billy S. briefed me for my first meeting with housemasters and my first Masters' Meeting. I promised both gatherings one thing: I was not going to burst in and make a lot of innovations straight away. I would sit and watch; and if, as might conceivably be, there were things I thought might be altered I would not make any changes until I had been there for a year. I was determined not to sacrifice their confidence and their support by being a young man in a hurry: after all, I probably had more time than most of them had. One detail sticks in the memory. Apparently it was part of my duty, on the first assembly of the school at the beginning of term, to read out in a clear public voice the whole of the School List form by form – I suppose as one way of announcing any promotions since the term before. I thought it prudent to rehearse the list, aloud, at the first housemasters' meeting, lest I should commit the unforgivable *gaffe* of pronouncing a boy's name incorrectly in public. I stumbled over one, a surname I had never encountered before, and asked where the stress came in its pronunciation. The boy's housemaster, a Cambridge Classic, gruffly and weightily said, 'It's a dactyl, Headmaster.'

Before the school as a whole had to be faced there was the arrival of the inmates of the School House; for in those days the Headmaster had a boys' boarding house as well as his wider responsibilities. Increasingly, since those days, headmasters have not had boarding houses; and I am sure there are strong arguments in favour of this trend. I can only say that for me, coming as I did with no knowledge of the inner workings of a boarding school, having a boys' house was an absolutely essential element in my learning and experience. To have fifty of them, from the top form to the bottom, under our own roof; to see and hear them about the place all day; to eat with them every day at school lunch; to walk round the dormitories every night as they were going to bed; to have individuals coming in every evening after House Prayers about something or other – all this gave me the opportunity of seeing in microcosm what the whole school was like. There is always a danger that a headmaster normally sees only two lots of boys, the best, in the persons of his prefects and Sixth Forms, and the worst, the naughty ones who are in trouble; the vast majority of the population may escape him altogether, the normal ones who achieve neither great position nor delinquency. It is not for me to pontificate; and I do not underestimate the difficulties, unknown in those days, which headmasters now endure. I can only say that I am very glad that I had the chance of getting to know a cross-section of 'the ordinary boy'. Of course, a resident House Tutor took off my plate the normal administrative chores, and a gallant wife looked after the housekeeping and the domestic staff. But the final responsibility for those fifty boys was mine, in a more direct and intimate sense than my responsibility for the other four hundred and fifty, ultimate as that properly was.

And on a never-to-be-forgotten evening they arrived. Mostly they came by special trains, either from London or from the northwest; six times a year, at the beginning and end of each term, the

end-of-the-line railway station at Uppingham came to life. Very
few came by car, and these were chiefly new boys whose parents
wanted to bring them and see their housemasters about Tommy's
idiosyncracies or Michael's sensitiveness. My House Tutor was an
old hand, whose only failing was that he was so used to School and
House routine that he could not give an account of it to a new-
comer; my House Captain was less than ten years younger than I
was, and he took me in hand; he assured me that everything would
be all right. Fortunately, the School House was going through a
period of prosperity and success, both academically and athletically,
so we had no corporate qualms. They all looked cheerful, lively,
clean and bright as I faced them for the first time at House Prayers;
and so far as I know I dropped no bricks.

One item in that ceremony came as a surprise, though I hope I did
not show it. The boys' dining-room, where House Prayers took
place, was separated from the 'private side' dining-room by a door.
When House Prayers occurred this door was kept open and the
domestic staff assembled in the 'private side' dining-room to take
part, in the best Victorian family prayers style. It diffidently emerged,
from an embarrassed House Captain, that the boys were accustomed
to seeing the Head Man's wife in the doorway. No doubt she had in
the past been there to intercept any ocular contact between boys and
domestics. I ventured to ask my guide and mentor, Billy S., if we
had to perpetuate this nonsense. He exploded in laughter. They had
had no idea that the School House had continued to be so explicitly
Victorian; certainly this quaint practice had no place in any other
house. So I broke my promise about no innovations – to the great
relief of the domestic staff, who, as we learnt, had always had to
break off the washing-up at a particularly inconvenient moment in
order to attend these blasted Prayers.

On the first ordinary weekday of term there was another innovation in my own life and habits. In those days we had Early School,
one period of teaching before breakfast. That meant that I, conducting School Prayers in Hall, had to be awake enough to read alternate
verses of a Psalm at 7.30 a.m. In Oxford my first pupil had normally
paraded at ten o'clock; and I had not reckoned to be conscious until,
after breakfast in pyjamas and dressing-gown, I had dressed and
organised myself for a ten o'clock start. In serious fact this was a real
problem for my first year at Uppingham. It was no good going to

bed earlier; I could not get to sleep until my Oxford normal of one or two o'clock. So I lived on short nights throughout that first Summer Term.

I had inherited a secretary, who lived in the house and was by Scottish nature an early riser. The morning mail was collected from the village post office in a private bag by the houseman on his way in and brought to me by 7.30 a.m. So if I was not teaching in Early School we could answer the day's letters before breakfast. This also was in accordance with tradition, because my predecessor had told me that throughout his time he had replied to every letter on the day he had received it.

One of the major joys was teaching – and not only because it provided a sanctuary from the telephone. I engaged myself with the Classical Upper Sixth for Greek Testament and for a Greek play, and with the Science Upper Sixth for what we broadly called 'English'. The former, it may as well be admitted, strayed beyond construe into amateur exegesis. The Epistle to the Hebrews is pretty tough meat to share with a dozen intelligent boys. The latter was more relaxed. I started by reading to them samples of English poets and asking them to decide, after three weeks, which one they would like to hear more of. In one memorable year they opted for Milton. So in the course of one term I read aloud the whole of *Paradise Lost*. I well know that by modern fashions they themselves should have done the reading. But I could not conscientiously entrust that majestic poetry to their immaturity; and I believe that they, and I am sure that I, became the richer for that experience.

So we settled into a new pattern of living, being mercifully young and resilient. Half-way through that first term our first-born arrived, hurrying (as throughout his life he did) to get born on his father's birthday. He was the first baby to be born in the School House for, they said, fifty years. So he was an event, not only in the school but in the neighbourhood as well. In this respect, as in some others, he was a-typical. One of the major differences between a boys' boarding school and a girls' boarding school was that in the former there were always wives and families round the place, whereas in the latter there were, presumably, no males except the gardeners. Things are different now when Roedean, for example, has a headmaster. One of the entertaining influences of our small son was the intense interest he aroused in the boys of the School House. Tough rugger forwards were to be seen tip-toeing across the lawn to his pram to peep in. For them he was a baby brother by proxy. My House Captain at lunch one day, when the child was four or five months old, cleared his throat and asked with strangled voice and obvious worry if Jeremy was all right. I said he was, so far as I knew, why? 'Well, sir, he doesn't seem to be talking much yet, does he?' He little knew how completely the child would rebut, in later years, this friendly but misplaced concern.

There was plenty to do – in the classroom, in the House, entertaining and being entertained round the County. There was one entirely new experience, addressing the school in Chapel. Visiting bishops always maintained that they were terrified of preaching in school chapels, where the congregations were, they said, the most critical they ever encountered. I replied that it was easy for them: they came, delivered their standard public school sermon, and went, whereas I had to utter on the first Sunday of term and live with it for thirteen weeks. One piece of advice I ventured to give them, after a little experience – 'Never read a written-out sermon in a school chapel: if they see you turning over the pages they will stop listening.' There were occasional embarrassments. There was the bishop who contrasted the good fortune of his congregation, born in happy homes and brought up in a Christian school, with the lives of those unfortunate babies who were born in brothels. Fortunately, he was inaudible beyond the first three rows, so very few were in a position to wonder about his experience or his ignorance. It was very different with another distinguished Old Uppinghamian cleric. He preached a rousing, dramatic sermon, full of local topographical knowledge. 'One Sunday when I was a boy here, as it might be you or you or you, I was on my Sunday afternoon walk with my friend of that time, as it might be you or you or you; and over there to the south by Ridlington the veil of the finite was rent, and divinity shone through.' And so on: stirring stuff. Two years later, like a fool, I invited him again. After fifteen seconds it became clear that we were to have the same sermon again. And we did, except that this time, as they were walking 'over there to the west by Beaumont Chase the veil of the finite was rent and divinity shone through'. I consoled myself with the reflection that nearly half the school had come since his last visit. But in the dormitories that night my House

Captain, a pretty-well-on-the-spot Yorkshireman, asked if he could ask me a question. 'Of course: what?' 'Sir, where exactly was it that the veil of the finite was rent?'

About that time there was another development not unconnected with Chapel. For more than forty years Uppingham had had a vague connection with the Mersey Mission to Seamen. Twice a year a Missioner from Liverpool came and told us what a splendid job was done by the Flying Angel throughout the seaports of the world. I did not doubt this; but I did wonder what in particular it had to do with the boys of Uppingham School. More critically, I could not help resenting the notion that the social conscience or altruistic benevolence of the school (if that was what was supposed to be involved) should be thought to be satisfied by listening to reminiscences of Rio or B.A. and then dropping a coin in a collection bag. If we were going to do this sort of thing I would much prefer that we did it through a more local and intimate concern.

By fortunate chance the opportunity cropped up on our doorstep. The steel firm of Stewarts and Lloyds had just begun an enormous development at the Northamptonshire village of Corby, ten miles away from us on the other side of the Welland valley, on the revolutionary basis, as I vaguely understood it, of bringing the coal to the ironstone instead of taking the ironstone to the coal. Corby in those days was just being transformed from a remote village to an industrial town. Stewarts and Lloyds had planned the whole thing in advance. They had built houses, churches, shops, playing-fields before they brought in their work force, largely from Glasgow. Their chairman happened to be an Old Uppinghamian, his son happened to be Captain of the School, one of the executive directors happened to live in Uppingham. In their careful pre-planning the firm had overlooked one thing. They had made admirable welfare provision for their workers. But they had somehow not noticed that their workers might have children. They had made no provision for anything like boys' clubs. Soon after the immigration of workers occurred this oversight became screamingly obvious. Gradually we got together, and a useful joint operation emerged. Stewarts and Lloyds would provide a building and pay the salary of a warden: we would produce a dozen boys each evening for the normal purposes of sports and games and general club activities; and each week-end a bunch from each end would spend twenty-four hours with the other. Individual masters put in a great deal of selfless work; individual workers at Corby, at all levels, did the same; and in a very short time the Uppingham-Corby Club was in practical operation. The fundamental principle of the whole enterprise, I affirmed, was that each of the partners was in it to learn from the other. The inaugural exercise was a joint camp of twelve or fifteen young men from each end. Photographs reveal that when you see them in congenial surroundings, all naked from the waist up, you cannot tell which come from which end. As anybody might have known.

Just about that time there were prophecies of gloom and doom about the future of the public schools. How could they survive in the increasingly difficult economic situation? How would any parents be able to afford constantly rising fees? (There is no wonder that some of us, forty years later, have a feeling of *déjà vu*.) These fears seemed, and seem, to be based on the mistaken view that there is in England a 'public school class'. Obviously it will happen that some parents who themselves attended independent schools will be unable, from lack of financial success or from the incidence of taxation, to send their sons to their own old schools. What seemed to be overlooked was the number of fathers who had not been at such schools but wanted to send their sons to them. Their motives may have been snobbish or prudential or even academic; but it could not be denied that such fathers existed. I conducted a simple enquiry. 'Was your father at Uppingham or some similar school?' The answer was 'Yes' for between thirty and thirty-five per cent. Indeed, we reckoned that we could tell from the applications for future entries which parts of the national economy were booming. I was surprised, at one moment, at the number of applications on behalf of sons of dentists, until I learnt that dentists had had a salary award.

Nevertheless, we had our financial problems. There was no serious shortage of boys, but their fees simply covered recurrent expenses. And in fact although some houses were over-subscribed, not all the houses were full, either because some were more modern than others or because some were nearer to the school buildings than others, or because some housemasters were more acceptable to parents than others. We invented a 'pool system', which ensured that those houses which had more boys than an agreed number should pay the house fees of the supernumeraries into a pool from which those houses which were below full complement should draw – Communism in the public schools in the Thirties. Uppingham was not a school with massive endowments. My predecessor had carried out a substantial building programme over the years; but there was very little money for me to spend on some of the things I thought necessary. I did succeed in getting rid of the earth-closets I had inherited in four of the boarding houses and in building a new sanatorium to supersede a Victorian villa with the stagnant pond of Thring's aviary in its garden. (The first service I attended in the School Chapel was the funeral of a boy who had died there during the Easter holidays.) It is lack of capital rather than of reliable income which puts the brakes on a school; and one cannot too often combine an increase in fees with appeals for capital expenditures.

After a couple of years the outside world began to impinge. Isolated though it was, Uppingham was not entirely exempt from what was happening outside; and in the course of 1936 there began to be strange rumours about the King. We heard them only at third or fourth hand, from visiting parents or overnight lecturers; but they grew in volume and eventually came to present a real difficulty in such an 'Establishment' establishment as a public school. At last the news officially broke, and one of the trickiest jobs I have ever had to do was to assemble the whole school on the evening of December 10th, 1936, and explain to them that King Edward VIII had abdicated. It was not our business to have any views about his action or the reasons for it. The point was that the Duke of York had succeeded him, and we now had a new King, to whom our loyalty and allegiance were henceforth due.

It was not long before darker clouds loomed. Masters who were commissioned in the JTC had obvious obligations in the event of war. Through the machinery of the Headmasters' Conference schools which were in 'safe' areas made their offers to take schools who would have to be evacuated – all in the deepest secrecy. Munich came and went, with all its tensions, and we all breathed again, but prematurely; and it became clear in the early months of 1939 that existing provisional plans would have to be completed. We all attended Red Cross lectures to learn how to deal with bombs and gas; the biggest room in each boarding house was so equipped as to be gas-proof, despite the warnings of our science masters that if all the inhabitants of a house were so immured they would die from

75

lack of oxygen without any assistance from enemy action; during the summer holidays gangs of volunteers dug trenches in the gardens of each house, which in the end were never used, because the outside chance of a bomb came to be regarded as a better bet than almost certain deaths from pneumonia.

Arrangements to receive our evacuee school went furiously ahead, under a cloak of complete secrecy and anonymity. Nobody was allowed to know which school it was except the Chairman of the governing body and myself; and housemasters simply had to take it on trust from me that there would be such a school and that my proposals for their accommodation were such and such. In the village itself there was precious little spare accommodation and since the heart of Rutland was an obvious 'reception area' it was necessary to enlist the good offices of local billeting officers to reserve it for our visitors. Eventually, towards the end of the summer holidays I was allowed to come clean and inform masters and parents that the school was Kingswood, from Bath, whose buildings were being taken over by the Admiralty. Kingswood boys would sleep in all our spare-rooms and house sick-rooms; the age-old Uppingham tradition that each boy had a study of his own would have to go, so that our visitors had somewhere to sit and work; an abandoned boarding house in the High Street was to be re-opened and made over to them; the occupants of one boarding house of ours would be scattered round other houses and it lent to Kingswood; one major classroom block would be put at their disposal and we would revert to our former habit of teaching in house dining-halls; their Chapel services would be at different times from ours; their games and ours would have to be on the same pitches at staggered times; our gymnasium would become their dining-hall, with kitchens urgently added; and so on. The reactions of masters, parents and boys were exemplary. The only serious protest came from three members of the governing body, who demanded a special meeting to censure the Chairman and the Headmaster for entering into all these commitments without the authority of the full Board. The meeting was duly held and they were duly routed, largely by Claude Blagden's statesmanship and partly because their spokesman, in an opening address which took forty minutes, treated the two defendants as if they were on trial at the Old Bailey.

The Headmaster of Kingswood was A. B. Sackett, who had been

with the Lancashire Fusiliers at Gallipoli in the First World War. His achievement in keeping Kingswood not only alive but splendidly flourishing throughout the long years they spent at Uppingham is one of the major epics of British headmastering. His colleagues and boys had been used to a fairly compact manner of life, and they were now scattered in dozens and half-dozens round the school houses, hotels and private houses of Uppingham. They were indeed in exile, as Uppingham itself had been when Thring removed the whole school temporarily to Borth to escape from the inadequate sanitary arrangements of the Uppingham of his day. But Thring had not had to cope with the problems which inevitably arise from the cohabitation of two schools in the buildings of one. It was made a good deal easier in our case by the fact that the two schools were so different. We were just on five hundred, they were just under three hundred; the home backgrounds of ours were on the whole more prosperous than theirs; they were on the whole more hardworking than we were, because their futures depended more directly on their own efforts; and the denominational difference was not entirely irrelevant. If the two schools had been more alike there must necessarily have been – as in some other war-time juxtapositions there were – rivalries, jealousies and even resentments. These we were spared.

Sackett used as his office what had until then been my wife's sitting-room in the School House; so during the working day he and I were ten yards apart, using the same front door (but, mercifully, different telephone lines) and therefore in almost continuous communication. Twice, in the five years we worked together, we lost our tempers with each other, about some triviality or other. Both times, after shouting furious invective at each other for two minutes, we simultaneously burst into laughter.

The war, phoney and real, went on. Nights were disturbed. In the early days the air-raid warning system was rather primitive. When there was an Alert it was telephoned to the local post office exchange. There, mercifully, was a human being, not an automatic machine or an STD apparatus. He immediately informed me. I then telephoned four 'Sector Wardens'. The boarding houses at Uppingham were scattered, so I had designated the senior housemaster in each topographical area for this duty. It was his business to go, on foot, to the other houses in his area and rouse the housemasters – not an attractive liturgy at three o'clock in the morning. Equally it was his duty to inform his colleagues when I had transmitted the 'Green' which permitted everybody to go back to bed. Once the system broke down. The Sector Warden did his stuff about the Alert. As he tottered back to his house I telephoned 'Green'; and he tumbled thankfully into bed. As dawn broke one of his neighbours, who had kept his boys up all night, wandered angrily round to see what was going on. A rain of pebbles hit the bedroom window of the Sector Warden. He woke, ran to the window and opened it. A second hail of pebbles took him in the face, but that was nothing to his colleague's invective.

Later on, in more sophisticated times, there was a local air-raid siren which was perched on the roof of the School Tower, twenty yards from our bedroom window. It was said that we were on the boundary of the East Coast district for air-raid alarms, and it was hinted that just to be on the safe side the zealous operators included us in every 'Amber' that came along. After three awakenings a night we were not at our brightest when we got up in the dark, put on our LDV armlets and cycled a couple of miles to catch the German parachute-troops who were expected with each dawn. If I was lucky I was on the same watch as a local doctor who brought with him the appropriate amount of cherry brandy. We were not entirely clear what we were to do if the enemy came. We began to envy those who had been called up and were having a nice quiet time somewhere in the Army: but headmasters were sternly discouraged from leaving their posts.

Food rationing was a serious problem. We dug, like mad, for victory. But five hundred growing boys were difficult to feed, especially when good filling stuff like potatoes and, later, bread were restricted. The local rationing authorities did their best for us and house cooks worked marvels; but it was a tricky time. Housemasters' wives went gleaning for their hens behind the harvest and shelled peas while they watched cricket matches on the Upper. The rationing of other items of hitherto normal consumption had pleasanter consequences. Members of my governing body came to meetings on horseback, traps, pony-carts and even victorias jingled along the Rutland roads; village boys re-learnt the ancestral skill of holding horses' heads while the ladies did their shopping; and one County wife borrowed my goalkeeping pads for self-protection while she milked an obstreperous cow.

And then the war came straight to me. In the middle of December

1940 my morning mailbag contained a letter from the Air Ministry on that Cambridge-blue coloured notepaper which indicates a fairly high level of correspondent. The Air Ministry was considering some changes in the education and training of young men who aspired to be pilots in the Royal Air Force; they would like to discuss these proposals with a certain number of headmasters; if I was going to be in London within the next week or two could I call in at Adastral House to talk things over? My first reaction, before breakfast after a disturbed night, was peevish. I looked at a pile of five hundred reports which had to be written before the end of term; I had on my mind the complications of getting eight hundred boys away for their Christmas holidays on a single railway line; and anyway what did I know about training RAF pilots or navigators or air-gunners or anybody else, being easily the least mechanically-minded head-master then in business? Let Air Marshals get on with their job and leave me alone to do mine. Bad temper evaporated in the course of the day; but it was not succeeded by any great enthusiasm. How-ever, I supposed I ought not to withhold my invaluable counsel in the nation's desperate days. So I grudgingly replied that sometime next week, after the end of term, I would come and see whoever it was that wanted to see me.

The Air Marshal, Guy Garrod, was quite different from what I had expected. He had read Greats at Oxford, he was a violinist and an international rifle shot. In no time he and his civil servant, Folliott Sandford, got to work on me. I was given no chance of ask-ing many questions, or indeed of answering any, before I was whisked off to lunch and then suddenly confronted with the straight question: would I come to the Air Ministry for six months from January 1st to take charge of a national campaign to boost the num-bers of boys who would come forward for the RAF, from school or from work, with a good deal of their preliminary training already behind them? It would involve collaboration with schools, local education authorities, industry and the already existing Air Defence Cadet Corps. The Service side of things would be looked after by a high-ranking RAF officer as Commandant: my job would be on the civilian side, with the title of Director of Pre-entry Training. I protested that I knew nothing about RAF training, and hinted that their letter to me had been a little, well, disingenuous. I was told something of the shortages and of the desperate position we might soon be in; and the mixture of buttering-up and arm-twisting went on. But I was a headmaster, officially and sternly urged to stay at his post; what would my governing body say if I left my school and my house at practically no notice for a job which dozens of people could do better than I could? The cajolery continued. The Secretary of State was anxious to make an announcement before Christmas. My mention of my governing body reminded the Air Marshal that he and my Chairman had been contemporaries at Bradfield. Would I at least return home *via* Peterborough that afternoon and talk it over with him?

In a daze I arrived at the Bishop's Palace at Peterborough that evening to see my Chairman. It could be (I never asked) that there had been some telephonic conversation between the Air Marshal and the Bishop while I was on my way. By the time I had finished my narrative his mind was clear. The decision was, of course, mine; but he had no doubt that the governing body would release me, if the Secretary of State so requested and if I decided that I ought to go. We discussed what we should do about the school and the house in the event of my so deciding. I made my way across country to an anxious wife. We talked half-way through the night. Next morning I rang up my Air Marshal and two days later I was summoned to see the Secretary of State, Sir Archibald Sinclair.

He was at his most gracious, courteous and suave. After half an hour it was clear that we could not possibly win the war unless I, and nobody else, took on this imperative national obligation. I did in fact know something of the RAF's manpower problems, because Weldon was working as a temporary civil servant in the Air Ministry and he had happened to be staying with us at Uppingham while the Battle of Britain was actually on. So I knew that that had been 'a damned nice thing – the nearest run thing you ever saw in your life'. In short, there was nothing I could conceivably do but accept Sinclair's invitation. Fortunately, as I had agreed with my Chairman, there was a man on the spot at Uppingham who could perfectly well carry the place while I was away, P. F. Saunders, universally respected by his colleagues and by boys, calm, unruffled, experienced and shrewd. Similarly, my House Tutor could look after the School House. The Chairman saw no difficulty in my leaving my wife and family in the School House, for which she would continue to carry the domestic responsibility.

Defensive measures in 1941.
Jeremy (*right*), Michael Sackett and cousin
Sally at Uppingham

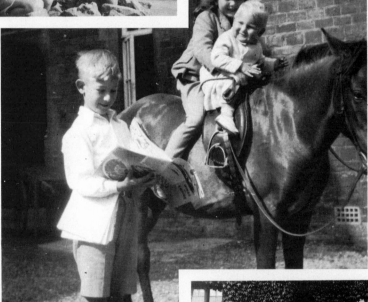

Jeremy, Priscilla and Daniel, 1943

Jeremy was the first baby to be
born in the School House at
Uppingham in fifty years, 1934

With Cyril Alington
at Shrewsbury, 1946

King Peter of Yugoslavia (*centre*, in uniform) at
an inspection of the ATC, 1941

All this was, at this stage, heavily secret – Heaven knows why. The secrecy was badly dented while we were innocently eating our Christmas dinner. An RAF despatch-rider came roaring up the High Street, blinded in under the Tower and swept to a screaming halt outside our front door. He bore the official invitation from the Air Council and the text of the announcement which the Secretary of State would shortly make. That is not the way to keep secrets in an inquisitive village like Uppingham; and I heard all kinds of rumours during the next forty-eight hours. On 1st January, 1941, I became Director of Pre-Entry Training in the Air Ministry, with a brief which was a bit woolly at the edges. A year later, the original six months having been extended to twelve, I went back to Uppingham.

There is no need to recount here the history of the Air Training Corps; it has been told, officially and unofficially, more than once. There was to be a public announcement by the Secretary of State on January 9th, and the ATC was to be formally constituted on February 1st, with His Majesty the King as Air Commodore-in-Chief. So I had exactly one month to make all the necessary contacts in the educational world, to frame at least the outlines of policy for a national organisation, to launch the inevitable public relations campaign, and, not least, to find my way about the Air Ministry and the Royal Air Force. I remained a civilian, and a temporary one at that. From time to time during the year I spent there it was suggested that I should go into uniform; and I am sure this was kindly meant by those who suggested it. I always declined, and when they asked my reasons I always gave the same reply: 'As I am, just a headmaster on temporary loan, I can, if I feel like it, talk to Air Marshals on more or less equal terms, with a pipe in my mouth and my hands in my pockets; I couldn't do that if I were dressed as an Air Commodore.' There is a lot to be said for preserving one's amateur status inside a highly hierarchical professional organisation.

There were all sorts of problems. Some were simply mechanical, like signing on the same day 850 letters to the headmasters of every independent and grammar school in the United Kingdom, or finding out the proper way to approach each lord lieutenant and mayor. Others were more technical, concerning the actual syllabuses which units of the ATC should follow in the training which was preparatory to their admission to the RAF. Yet others were technical in another sense, involving commissioning into the RAFVR school-teachers whose proficiencies were mathematical rather than aeronautical. Others again involved the relationship of a 'closed' school squadron to a local municipal Wing, or the status of already existing University Air Squadrons, or the possibility of inter-service friction if the ATC should seem to be stealing boys from the Army Cadet Force, or the danger that the whole idea of pre-entry training in mathematics and physics might seem intolerably bookish to boys who were passionately impatient to fly aeroplanes or shoot down Germans. And all this against a background of desperate urgency at one of the bleakest moments of the war. We, a staff of four at the beginning, were nearly overwhelmed. In the first month 110,000 recruits were enrolled, in over eight hundred separate units; by the middle of the summer there were said to be 190,000 of them.

We survived, with the unfailing backing of the Secretary of State and his Parliamentary Under-Secretary, Harold Balfour, and of their civil servants. The real responsibility was carried by Garrod, as Air Member for Training, who had to sell this rather unconventional idea to his Air Council colleagues, to justify the service manpower required to carry it out, and to keep up our own morale when things got a bit more than we could take. I saw him every day: we went together on visits to units all over the country; and his patience never failed. He would switch without affectation or strain from some problem of inter-service politics to asking me to repeat the Latin limerick I had told him last week, and he could still remember some of the lines of his part in the Bradfield Greek play. He later became godfather to our second son, Mark, who, according to his elder brother, by now at the age of eight an authority on aircraft recognition, was so called because he was a Wolfenden Mark III.

There were also some personal problems for me. I had to find somewhere in London to live. I had since Magdalen days been a member of the United University Club, in Suffolk Street. The rules about long-term occupancy of bedrooms were fairly strict. But I was permitted to stay there 'until I could find something else'. I stayed there for twelve months. As the year wore on and nightly bombing became routine it was a fairly hot spot, and the morning walk down the Strand to Adastral House provided daily evidence of what had happened the night before. Practically everything round us was hit, hotels, banks, shops, and we never knew, as we got up in the morning, whether there would be water or gas. We developed a blasé indifference, having long ago decided that if we were going to be blown to bits we would rather be warm and comfortable in bed when we were. Only twice did we get up in the middle of the night, when it was just too noisy to sleep. The roster of fire-watching, with other members and with the Club servants, produced a sort of affection for the place which shared discomfort and danger engender.

At the Club during these months I made two new friends. On most mornings at breakfast was Edward Bridges, recovering from a violent night and preparing for a thick day. Being Secretary to the Cabinet and Head of the Civil Service was, in the days of Winston Churchill and the nights of bombs, no sinecure. He sat alone and nobody disturbed him. But after breakfast we sometimes exchanged words, and there were laid then the foundations of a relationship which in later and happier days was of immense benefit to the University of Reading. The other new friend was C. P. Harvey. He was a barrister whose other skills were billiards and brilliant light verse. I still possess the manuscripts of poems which describe me as a Companion of the Breakfast Egg or narrate with mordant astringency the meeting of the Premier and the President of the United States or the declaration of our War Aims. And he taught me a lot about billiards and snooker while the table shook with the reverberation of bombs and anti-aircraft guns.

I reckoned to get down to Uppingham for about one week-end in three, bombs permitting. When I was there I was, of course, a private citizen visiting my family, not a headmaster. Philip Saunders and I had an entirely uncomplicated relationship: he was Headmaster until I came back. But it was a great solace to see wife and children from time to time and to get an uninterrupted night's sleep, which the siren on the Tower totally failed to invade. I began to understand why people who live and work in London like to have a country cottage for the week-ends.

Meanwhile the ATC grew and grew. I attended, at my Minister's shoulder, a meeting of the Home Affairs Committee of the Cabinet, with John Anderson in the chair and, by a happy chance of seating, Ernest Bevin just in front of me. I saw and heard for the first time, from the overt proceedings and his muttered commentary, how affairs of State are conducted. I waited upon Stafford Cripps and

83

Clement Attlee, on behalf of my own Secretary of State, and I came to appreciate Permanent Secretaries like Arthur Street, who, if anybody did, gave his life for his country. King George VI came to visit an ATC camp at Halton; the two teenage Princesses came over from Windsor to a wartime lunch in an RAF Officers' Mess. At the end of lunch we were offered cheese, biscuits – and butter. The first words I ever heard my present Sovereign speak, in a clear fifteen-year-old voice, were 'Butter? We don't get that at home.' There were television interviews and sessions with representatives of Commonwealth and foreign governments who thought they might institute something of the same sort. There were inspections and reviews all up and down the country – my first and last public appearance on the sacred turf of Cardiff Arms Park was for a vast rally of the ATC units of South Wales – and there were almost daily conversations with the top people in the Board of Education, with our Scottish colleagues, with the Ministry of Labour and National Service, and with the contractors who were lamentably slow in producing uniforms with the right buttons.

So the year drew towards its end, with no slackening of pressure but with a staff now fully capable, in number and quality, of coping. There were friendly suggestions that I might stay on in the Air Ministry as a civil servant. But I wanted to get back to Uppingham; and, anyhow, I was under clear obligation to the governing body who had treated me so generously. The same was the answer to two schools which put out feelers about my succeeding their incumbent headmasters. There was a splendid Air Council farewell lunch, with the Secretary of State to pronounce an elegant valediction; and there were less formal good-byes on the top floor of Adastral House. It had been quite a year.

Uppingham was in fine flourishing form when I got back, as I had known it would be. It was a joy to be there again, in familiar surroundings and routines, to catch up on a year's new boys, and to discover, sometimes with some surprise, which of those I had not seen for twelve months had become the swells of the place. Shortages and rationings were no less stringent. Travelling restrictions made us look for less distant opponents on football fields and there was a shocking day when we were beaten, at home, by Stowe, after one of the most glorious games of Rugby football ever seen by man. Watching a school match in the company of the headmaster of the enemy was always a test of nerves and manners. When it was Hugh Lyon from Rugby pleasure in the contest was greatly increased; we sat side by side in the special Headmaster's box in the pavilion exchanging with total good humour ridiculous Fourth-form ruderies which were no doubt an indication of tension. It was not always so. Another headmaster, on his home ground, announced at half-time that he was going for a walk round. When I innocently suggested that I might come with him, he snapped, 'No: you stay where you are.'

I began to get involved in national committees. In the summer of 1942 Rab Butler asked me to be Chairman of the Board of Education's Youth Advisory Council. In November 1939 the Board had issued its historic Circular 1486, entitled 'The Service of Youth'. Up to that time the leisure activities of young people, in Boys' Clubs, Girl Guides, the Boys' Brigade, and so on, had been the concern of voluntary organisations. The circumstances of wartime, with the black-out, the requisitioning of club premises, and the disappearance into the armed forces of many who had been the leaders in these activities, made it extremely difficult for these organisations to carry on their work, while at the same time those very circumstances made that work all the more necessary. The Government therefore decided that it must take a hand, to supplement the voluntary agencies. In a field which was regarded as being, in the widest sense, educational, it followed the established practice of this country, that the Government does not operate directly but conveys its policies and intentions to the local education authorities, putting on them the responsibility for action. Circular 1486 therefore urged on authorities the creation of properly constituted Youth Committees, with representatives of the principal voluntary organisations, teachers, religious denominations and industry, to bring about 'the close association of local education authorities and voluntary bodies in full partnership in a common enterprise'. A National Youth Committee was appointed to advise the President and to provide central guidance and leadership.

This Circular, born of bombs and black-out, was epoch-making. For the first time a government undertook a direct responsibility for youth welfare. And it initiated a partnership between the statutory arm and the voluntary bodies which has persisted, through various vicissitudes, to the present day. Of course nobody in that atmosphere of crisis and urgency could foresee all the complications; and I suspect that nobody foresaw that the foundations then hastily laid would come to support the weighty structure which by now has been built upon them. But it was a remarkable initiative for a government to take when it was pretty heavily occupied with other affairs.

When Rab became President of the Board in 1941 he slightly altered the pattern at the centre. Instead of a National Youth Committee, with the Parliamentary Secretary as Chairman, he appointed a Youth Advisory Council of some twenty members drawn from the L E As, the uniformed Cadet Forces, the Churches and the established Youth organisations; and he asked me to be its Chairman. It was not his intention that we should concern ourselves with the day-to-day running of the partnership between the statutory and the voluntary; that was by now launched and operating, with some stresses and strains but with the practical success which empirical improvisation sometimes achieves. Rather, he wanted us to look into the future and to speculate on two issues which had already presented themselves in the three years since Circular 1486. He therefore suggested that we should focus our attention on two main questions: What should be the position of the Youth Service in the education service after the war? and, What should be the future of the pre-service training organisations? We accordingly gazed into our collective crystal ball and produced in the summer of 1943 a report entitled *The Youth Service after the War*.

In the following year he gave us a new remit, to be yet more theoretical and speculative about the whole purpose and content of the Youth Service, and those words provided the title for our second report. Thirty years later it makes rather antiquarian reading. But at least it set out some thoughts on society's responsibility to its younger members – and theirs to it – which seem to have passed into the standard currency. This second enterprise, with some changes in the personnel of the Council, gave me the opportunity of meeting for the first time a young man named George Brown, then a District Officer of the Transport and General Workers' Union; we have kept in touch with each other, through all the changes and chances of this mortal life, ever since.

Meanwhile, the end of my projected ten years at Uppingham loomed. Apart altogether from any dogma about that, we began to have problems inside the home. By now we had four children, skilfully arranged in two pigeon-pairs, and their education had to be attended to. It was not so difficult to deal with the boys, because at the appropriate ages they could go to boarding preparatory schools. It was not so easy about the girls. While they were all younger we had organised a private collective nursery school for our own young and their contemporaries; and we were abundantly fortunate in the grounding which these youngsters received from two devoted and single-minded teachers. But when the girls outgrew that arrangement what were we to do? We were in a remote village in wartime. The village primary school was at the end of our garden: should they go to it? If they did, there was very little for them to learn that they had not been taught already: if they did not, would the young and 'progressive' headmaster be accused of social and academic snobbery? Worse, what would happen when they reached secondary school age? The nearest girls' school was Stamford, and a very good school it was; but it was a day school, and the daily journey there and back was not easy to organise with petrol rationing what it was.

These and other problems of conscience were solved from outside. I had already reminded my Chairman of the ten-year point when an approach came from Shrewsbury. It was not altogether easy. To move from one school to another is almost bound to give the impression that the one to which you go is in some sense or other 'better' than the one you are leaving. And, apart from that, was it fair to leave any school in the middle of all the problems of wartime? We decided to move. I did my best to explain, to colleagues, parents and boys, my point of view about this ten-year business; I rejected flatly any suggestion that Shrewsbury was a 'better' school than Uppingham; and I maintained that it was perhaps a positive advantage to Uppingham to find a new headmaster now rather than have to wait until the end of the war when there would be an enormous General Post on the departure of those many headmasters who had stayed on past retirement age to 'see it through'. Anyhow, it was better all round to go while some people seemed to regret your going than to stay so long that everybody was thinking 'In the name of God, go!' So we went.

6

Shrewsbury School
[1944]

It is not for nothing that the setting of Shrewsbury School is
traditionally known as 'the Site', for it must be one of the loveliest
in Britain. The school stands on a high bluff outside that great loop
of the Severn which almost encloses the town of Shrewsbury. Its
buildings are not particularly distinguished, but they are spaciously
disposed round a vast playing-field, 'the Common', with trees and
gardens in the foreground and the Welsh hills in the distance. The
original buildings in the town, opposite the Castle, were for pious
pilgrimage; but the migration in 1881 to the slopes of Kingsland
across the river provided a site healthier, more open and more free.

It is sometimes supposed that public schools are all pretty much
alike, and that apart from parental idiosyncracy of choice any boy
might as well go to any one as to any other. This is not so; and the
differences between Uppingham and Shrewsbury were more significant than their similarities. Shrewsbury was an Edward VI
foundation, with the names of Philip Sidney and Fulke Greville in
its original register: Uppingham was indeed Elizabethan in sheer
date, but its history really begins with the advent of Edward Thring
in 1853. There was a 'royal and ancient' thread running through the
whole fabric of Shrewsbury which was absent from the more
mercantile background of Uppingham. Thring had been more
concerned, in modern idiom, to give a fair deal to the ordinary boy
than to concentrate on the academic race-horses: Shrewsbury, with
a remarkable trio of headmasters in Butler, Kennedy and Moss, who
between them spanned a hundred and ten years in office, had
established a reputation for classical scholarship which persisted long
after they had gone. There were other differences, seemingly trivial
but not insignificant. Uppingham had no day-boys: Shrewsbury

had enough to constitute a separate house. Shrewsbury, with the
Severn at the bottom of School Bank, was a rowing school, which
reckoned to give a good account of itself annually at Henley; and,
unlike Uppingham, it played football with a round ball. The very
climate of the Severn valley was different from the invigorating
uplands of Rutland.

There were also, it quickly became apparent, differences in my
own particular job in the two schools. At Shrewsbury the Headmaster no longer had a boys' boarding house. The School House was
almost double the size of any other house and was internally divided
into two for inter-house competitions; so it would have been very
difficult for a headmaster to carry that as well as the school at large.
One consequence was that the Headmaster lived just off the Site, in
Kingsland House, a long low mellow brick Georgian house covered
by ancient wistaria, with a walled garden and an orchard dancing
with daffodils. It was a glorious house to live in, and our children
were lucky to be brought up in it. But the whole arrangement was,
from the Headmaster's point of view, a considerable change from
Uppingham. Not only did I not see my customary daily sample of
the ordinary boy; I physically lived away from the centre of gravity
of the school, with a walk across the Common in to school and out
home again for meals.

Which things were an allegory. At Uppingham I had inherited a
tightly-knit autocracy, where the authority of the Head Man was
apparent in the most trivial details. At Shrewsbury, or so it seemed
at first sight, the Headmaster was at best a constitutional monarch
intervening from time to time, mostly in matters of formality or
ceremony, while the actual running of the place was in the hands of
a highly competent body of masters and senior boys. A cruder way
of putting it would be that at Uppingham no boy was allowed to
deviate from regulations (or even, they said, blow his nose) without
express permission to do so, while at Shrewsbury everybody did
pretty much as he liked until somebody for some reason or other
told him to stop. Correspondingly, it looked as if my own personal
contribution ought to be different in the two different sets of
circumstances. At Uppingham it had been my business to do a
controlled relaxation (some said humanisation) of a pretty rigid
regimen: at Shrewsbury it seemed that a little more direction from
the centre could well be introduced without endangering the

spontaneity and independence of mind on which Salopians prided themselves. I expect that both masters and boys had been afraid that I should try to transplant and impose on them what they doubtless regarded as the restrictive habits of the other school; and I did catch a hint or two of these apprehensions. I had not, of course, intended anything of the kind. But I was concerned to see that their valued liberties did not fall apart into chaos.

I started by laying on a weekly meeting with the school prefects (officially, Praepostors, abbreviated at Uppingham to 'Pollies', at Shrewsbury to 'Postors'), as much to get to know them and to take the temperature of the place as for any more formal business. We met in the evening, not in a classroom but in the vast play-room at Kingsland House, and we talked for hours, they instructing me in the ancient mythologies and unwritten traditions and I trying to reassure them that I did not intend to pull the place to pieces and re-make it from scratch. It was an engaging process of mutual education. And the same sort of thing, *mutatis mutandis*, went on between myself and a splendid Cabinet of senior masters.

The war, of course, was still going on. Our nights were not disrupted, down on the Welsh marches, as violently as they had been in Uppingham or London. But senior boys could hardly be expected to concentrate on university scholarships when all they knew was that next month they would be in uniform; and week by week the terrible tally grew of those who had been here a few months ago and would never visit us again. Further, there were one or two staffing problems not unlike those I had experienced myself as a boy at school in the First War.

At first I simply took over my predecessor's teaching timetable, which consisted of Greek or Latin translation with the Classical Upper Sixth before breakfast. Towards the end of the first term one of the School Praepostors, in the course of supper at Kingsland House, protested that the Upper Sixth now spent much more time in school than they had done in the past. Puzzled, I asked how that could be, since I had in no way changed the timetable. 'No, sir, I know. But when you are taking us at half-past seven, you are in at half-past seven. Until this term we knew that we didn't need to arrive until about a quarter to eight.' Punctuality seems a fairly ordinary requirement in a headmaster.

Later on, with a little more self-confidence, I ventured on a couple of mild experiments. I asked the masters who were collectively responsible for the Classical Upper Sixth if I could have that form for the whole of two solid days. They blinked and mildly asked what I had in mind. I said I would like to try doing a whole Greek play straight through, instead of translating a hundred lines a time at intervals of several days. I explained. First I would read a translation of the whole play, while they followed in the Greek; then each boy would translate a hundred lines previously allotted to him, as fast as he could; then I would read the translation of the whole thing again. So, I hoped, each boy would know one hundred lines thoroughly and all of them would have some acquaintance with the continuous action of the whole play. Anyhow, would they mind if I tried it? Obviously this was no substitute for the thorough and scholarly work which they did with the form, nor was it intended to be, but at least I should enjoy it and would they indulge me to this extent? With some misgivings they agreed; and I had the bliss of presenting the *Antigone* to a bunch of intelligent boys in a way which seemed to me not particularly revolutionary.

The other piece of mild pottiness occurred at the other end of the school. The man who took the bottom form for Latin was belly-aching about 'these nitwits who must have been doing Latin for years at their prep schools but never seem to get a single blasted sentence right.' I sympathised, perhaps rather tepidly. He asked if I could possibly some day spare the time to come and take them and see for myself. Of course I could. So one day I confronted a couple of dozen thirteen-year-olds who may have been as much alarmed at this sudden epiphany from on high as I was amused at my foolhardiness in straying so far outside my normal age-range and at the prospect of trying to lure these little chumps into getting a Latin sentence right, with their form master sitting at the back. I suggested that we might abandon, just this once, their book of English sentences arranged for translation into Latin and see if we could between us write some Latin off our own bats. After some dis-cussion we agreed that we would describe the previous week-end's visit of a party of boys from our Boys' Club in Liverpool: how we met them at the station, gave them lunch in houses, took them on the river, played cricket on the Common until everybody went to bed, and then filled Sunday before they went back home. Collec-tively we decided that the station was 'the place where the swift chariots stopped', cricket was 'a game in which this man throws a ball and his enemy hits it with wood'; meals, river, bed and Chapel called for less periphrasis. By the end of an hour we had produced fifteen lines of flawless Latin narrative. Some, of course, had contributed more than others: but we had broken through the barrier of never getting a Latin sentence right.

Cyril Alington had been Headmaster of Shrewsbury before he went to Eton, and the legends persisted – how after elegant Greek versifying in the morning with the Classical Sixth he would take a brilliant hundred off the First XI bowlers in the afternoon, or drift urbanely round the Common with a black straw hat under his arm and the invariable daisy between his lips. One of his more successful unorthodoxies had been to appoint as his secretary a young man named Neville Cardus, who had originally come to Shrewsbury as assistant to the cricket professional. But for one reason or another he had not been back to Shrewsbury for a good many years. There were still masters on the staff whom he had appointed, and they enthusiastically endorsed my plot that we should winkle him out of the Deanery at Durham, where he now lived, to come and preach in the Chapel – after all, there were Shrewsbury Fables before there were Eton Fables. It was arranged, and he came, accompanied by his wife, every inch a Lyttelton.

I had done a substantial build-up of him in the school, as one of the great names of our past. Old, silver-haired, still handsome, now rather lame, he made his way to the pulpit and preached. It was an almost complete flop. Either because he was out of the habit of talking to boys or because memories crowded too thick around him or just because he was tired he never got going at all. At dinner with us afterwards he was unusually quiet and asked if he might go to bed early. At breakfast next morning he said he had had a miserable night; he knew that he had 'failed'; was there anything he could do to try to put things right? I said nothing could be simpler. I explained that we now had School Prayers on Monday mornings not in Chapel but in a secular building, the eponymously-named Alington Hall, so that I could, if I wanted to, address the school on mundane administrative or disciplinary matters. Would he care to come, and talk to them for ten minutes on anything he wanted to say? He said he would be deeply grateful for the opportunity, if I did not mind risking a second failure. He came with me on to the platform; I said how honoured we were to have him there, and handed over to him. He sat on the edge of the table and just talked, for ten minutes. It was absolutely brilliant; the whole lot of us were spell-bound; and there might easily have been a standing ovation at the end. Not all men of his age and distinction realise when they have fallen short, and have the humility to admit it and then show the guts to make a century in the second innings after a duck in the first.

About this time I began to be involved in headmastering politics on the national scale. There was a Fleming Committee set up in 1942 and a subsequent Fleming Report. The general idea was a breaking down of the barriers of privilege which were held to encompass the public schools, an end to the simply financial qualification for entry, an opening up of this particular form of education to merit or desert or need. Spencer Leeson of Winchester was at that time Chairman of the Headmasters' Conference and the liberalism of the position which he and Robert Birley represented was decisive. The Fleming Report itself perhaps tried to go too far too fast. But for my part I was prepared to go at least as far and as fast as it. The substantial recommendation was that a minimum of twenty-five per cent of the places in independent boarding schools should go to boys who had spent not less than two years of their earlier education in the schools of the national system of education.

Irrespective of official decision some of us were prepared to try it. It should perhaps be recorded that the Fleming Committee was set up because the public schools asked for it, not because a government was seeking to impose 'democracy' on 'institutions of privilege'. Many of us wanted to see an element in our recruitment different from that which was traditional. We did, believe it or not, think that our schools had something valuable to offer; and we thought that what we had to offer ought not to be confined to those boys whose parents could afford to pay the inevitably high fees. We did not think that we were providing the answer to all the country's sociological problems or resolving for good and all the 'two nations' dichotomy.

I wrote to half a dozen Directors of Education whom I personally knew, and asked if they were prepared to take part in some such scheme. With varying degrees of enthusiasm, influenced perhaps by the degree of control which each had over his authority's Education Committee, they all agreed. So at Shrewsbury we started, in a very humble and unpretentious way, a scheme for 'Fleming Bursars'. The candidates were to be put forward to us by the local education authorities, on whatever basis might seem to them proper. I reserved the right to talk to the boys they submitted, and their parents, mainly to satisfy myself about what is nowadays called 'motivation'. The LEA paid the full fees, recovering some part on a means test which they, not we, operated. Some of them chose their candidates on academic grounds, others picked boys from broken homes. I was to have the final say in each case. I do not remember any case of disagreement between us.

What I do remember is a heartening example of common sense on the part of the School Praepostors. I told them, at one of our weekly sessions, what I had in mind. Next term there would be a dozen or so new boys who had not been through the normal prep schools but would be coming from LEA secondary schools; they would probably not have been away from home before; this was our small contribution towards realising the ideals of the Fleming Report. It was absolutely vital that it should work, because if this pioneering move of ours failed it would be disastrous to the whole idea. My question to them was: What do I say about all this to the School at large? (I knew what I intended to do, but I wanted to see how much the Praepostors' view might differ from mine.) We had an hour's lively discussion, of principles and details, and at the end the Head of the School summed it up: 'You don't say anything at all to the School. If you do, these chaps will be labelled as part of a sociological experiment, and therefore will be treated differently from everybody else. The whole point is that they should not be treated differently. So say nothing. Anyway we probably shan't be able to distinguish them from anybody else.' Which totally confirmed my intention.

There were no serious problems. Sometimes there had to be some extra coaching in Latin, but that was looked after by a team of volunteer masters; and anyhow extra out-of-school classes of this kind were not uncommon. Each housemaster, of course, knew which of his new boys were Fleming Bursars; I left it to him whether or not he should tell anybody else. One of them came in to me after the first week-end of one term, gurgling with laughter. 'My House Matron came to me last night, in a raging fury, which is unusual for her. She said, "I've often heard you complain about prep schools not teaching boys anything nowadays. At least they used to teach them to clean their own shoes and make their own beds. Apparently they don't even do that now. Young Snodgrass, who arrived last week, has obviously never made his bed in his life." Snodgrass, of course, is one of my this term's Fleming Bursars. I expect his Mum has always made his bed until now.' Several of them took their places in School teams, and the normal proportion of them became School Praepostors. I remember only one failure, a boy who left at sixteen because he had had enough. He was the only one whose parents, on the LEA means test, were in a position to pay the fees in full. We had not realised that this form of entry could be used as a means of jumping the queue of applications for places in a full school.

In 1945 I was elected Chairman of the Headmasters' Conference, initiated by my Uppingham predecessor, Edward Thring, for a two-year term. Wartime travel between Shrewsbury and London was neither comfortable nor reliable, and after a day of meetings in London it was a toss-up whether I should get back in time for First Lesson before breakfast. My senior colleagues had to do a fair amount of standing in for me; but they agreed that they would rather do that than the train journeys.

The Headmasters' Conference was considerably involved in the consequences of the 1944 Education Act, and although I resigned the chairmanship of the Youth Advisory Council in 1945 I continued to see a good deal of successive Ministers (as they now were) and their officials. The headmasters of Conference schools were especially interested in a startling innovation which the 1944 Act formulated in the words, 'In fulfilling their duties under this section, a local education authority shall, in particular, have regard ... to the expediency of securing the provision of boarding accommodation, either in boarding schools or otherwise, for pupils for whom education as boarders is considered by their parents and by the authority to be desirable.' Plenty of material for controversy was provided by those words, and the then Permanent Secretary, Sir Maurice Holmes, gathered together an informal group of headmasters and headmistresses to discuss them. We gradually sorted out what the words did, and did not, mean. They did not mean 'public schools for all' or put on a local education authority an obligation to pay for a boy to go to an expensive boarding school just because his parents felt like it. They did not mean that 'boarding accommodation' and 'public school' were synonyms. What they did mean, apparently, was that ordinary boys and ordinary girls should have the chance of spending at least part of their school life as boarders. Special schools already existed to deal with special cases of disability of mind or body; now we were to deal, besides, not with the subnormal or the defective or the delinquent but with the normal, typical, ordinary child, and that not only at secondary school age but at primary school age too, if this were 'desirable'.

What was not at all clear was what was to be the basis of selection. What were to be the grounds on which the parents and the authority should consider boarding to be 'desirable' for any particular boy or girl? The first clue seemed to be 'need': which children had the greatest need of boarding? Gradually and empirically a list of priority groups began to be established – children of broken homes, or of parents living abroad or living in such remote places that normal day school was impracticable. All these, it was argued, must have the opportunity of boarding if they were to receive the education which it was the duty of the authority to provide.

But none of these criteria paid any attention to the major requirement of the 1944 Act that a child's education should be determined by his own age, ability and aptitude. They were all based on the circumstances of the parents, not on the character, temperament, interests or ambitions of the children. Nor did the relevant section of the Act say anything about 'need'; it said 'desirable'. There might be thousands for whom a boarding education was desirable who could not be said to need it; there were nothing like enough boarding places for everybody for whom it might be desirable; and it was going to be very difficult to persuade any authority's rate-payers to spend five times as much money on one normal child as on another just because the parents and the authority thought it was desirable for one normal child rather than another to go a-boarding.

There was a hope in some quarters that this whole business would be dealt with nationally, by the Ministry, rather than locally, by the LEAs. But this was opposed, partly on the ground that it would in principle be contrary to the tradition that in Britain the operation of educational administration is not undertaken centrally but is devolved to the localities, partly on the ground that a considerable central bureaucracy would have to be created to do the job, but chiefly because some LEAs were opposed to the whole idea and would passionately resist having their children included in a national scheme which they believed to be fundamentally mistaken.

Whatever the reasons, the necessary support was not forthcoming for anything like full realisation of the Fleming plan. Some of the most distinguished schools in the country tried to make it work; and some of the most distinguished LEAs tried to make the necessarily invidious decisions about selection. But it was, of course, extremely expensive for the authorities, and that is probably the main reason why in most cases the arrangements gradually fizzled out. There were indeed Fleming Bursars at Shrewsbury when I left some years later; but the number of participating LEAs was by then dwindling rather than increasing. It remains true, thirty years later, that it was a good try, even if it did not wholly come off.

About this time another, totally different, interest began to develop. In the summer of 1942 I had been appointed (more properly, assumed) as a member of the Carnegie United Kingdom Trust. I had been slightly surprised, though obviously flattered, to receive an invitation to join the Trust, because it was signed by Lord Elgin, the then Chairman. I had had a slight tiff with him a year before while I was wearing my ATC hat, because he had protested about our commissioning one of his employees without consulting him. I had thought he was being slightly pompous, and he had doubtless thought that I had to be put in my place. Anyhow, it seemed that all was forgiven; and his invitation set me on a course which has provided more interest and given me more friends than any out-of-school activity in which I have indulged.

The Carnegie United Kingdom Trust, one of several such bodies created by Andrew Carnegie for various separate purposes, is an interesting example of how the independent Trusts in this country operate. It is by no means the wealthiest of them – it disposes of about £200,000 a year – but its mode of operation is what makes it remarkable. There are some thirty Trustees, some designated by the Corporation of Dunfermline, some nominated by the Fife County Council, and the remainder Life Trustees. Of these last about half are Dunfermline-based, solicitors, bank managers, doctors: the other half are, if the phrase may be forgiven, 'public figures' from South of the Border. Out of this body of thirty, eighteen compose an Executive Committee, which is a happy and effective blend of Scots and Southerners, approximately half and half. This Executive

Committee then gives birth to sub-committees. Two of these are permanent and continuous, a Finance and Buildings Committee, comprising the experts on these topics, and a Policy Committee, which consists of the conveners (Anglicé, chairmen) of the other sub-committees, plus one or two elder statesmen, or stateswomen. These other sub-committees are not permanent. The Trust determines its major fields of interest, and therefore of its spending, quinquennially. It always keeps up its sleeve a certain amount of money for annual disbursement on particular items which crop up urgently and on a once-and-for-all basis. But its major policies, in relation to libraries, village halls, music, drama, the countryside, or whatever, are undertaken on a basis of at least five years. And – here is the important point – the pattern of sub-committees is quinquennially altered to correspond. There may be, in one quinquennium, sub-committees in fields X, Y and Z. When, with a shift in the Trust's interests, those policies are terminated, so are the sub-committees, and new ones are invented to cover fields P, Q and R. The Trust is not lumbered for ever with sub-committees which have served their purpose. This flexibility, exercised by a review every five years of what should be the major activities of the Trust, is a salutary manifestation of vitality and of refusal to get fossilised.

The other important procedural point is that all the members of the Executive Committee are members of all the sub-committees. They all sit round the same table through the whole programme of sub-committee meetings, with the difference that each sub-committee has a different convener, a member who has made one particular field of the Trust's activities his, or her, own speciality. So everybody knows all that is going on, under the changing chairmanships of a series of comparative experts. This 'Committee of the Whole House' procedure ought to be more widely practised.

Just before I joined the Trust, it had ventured into the field of what was called 'Youth'. I have never much liked 'Youth' with a capital 'Y', especially when there is 'Spotlight on Youth' or 'Focus on Youth', for two reasons. First, it seems to suggest that there is a strip or band of years in a person's life which can be peeled off and looked at separately and in isolation from the years that come before and the years that come after. This is not so; and we should do better to emphasise the continuity of a person's growth from the cradle through childhood and adolescence to maturity rather than chop it up into bits with no before or after. Secondly, I have never seen 'Youth', any more than I have ever seen an income-bracket or a C-stream. I have, in my time, seen a good many young people, of various ages, in various contexts. I have seen an endless variety of individual Margarets and Michaels and Joans and Johnnies. What I have never seen is 'Youth'. However, if it is recognised and remembered that this word is an abstraction and that it is used just as shorthand for these millions of devastatingly different individuals, perhaps there is no harm in it; the harm comes in when the shorthand abstraction is used as if it were real. A further danger had been introduced by the phrase 'Service of Youth' in the Board of Education's Circular 1486. Nobody quite knew whether 'of' meant 'to or for' or 'by, with or from'.

Cynics have been heard to say that the old only take an interest in the young when the young stand between the old and an invader. Certainly there was a good deal of interest shown in the years at and after the end of the war, and it was natural and right that the Carnegie Trustees should share in that interest. They had always prided themselves, down the years, on their faithfulness to Andrew Carnegie's original instructions. He laid it down, sixty-odd years ago, that his benefaction should be used 'for the improvement of the well-being of the masses of the people of Great Britain and Ireland ... by such means as ... Trustees might from time to time select as best fitted from age to age for securing these purposes, remembering that new needs are constantly arising as the masses advance.' There is a decidedly olde-worlde ring about the phraseology; but the heart of the matter is there and generations of Trustees have faithfully sought to pioneer, to experiment, to switch from one area of activity to another in the knowledge that 'new needs are constantly arising'. If there was a new need in the field of Youth, as distinct from public libraries or church organs or village halls, the Trust saw a duty to try to help meet it. This was the origin of a policy which by the time it was wound up ten years later had provided equipment and furniture for over seven hundred youth clubs and youth hostels.

But it had done more than that. One of the joys of a Trust like Carnegie is that you never know, when you start something off, where it is going to end. This incursion into the field of 'Youth' had all sorts of unexpected consequences, some immediate, others more indirect. The Trust's practice of working in co-operation with national associations in any field of interest brings to light, or inspires, projects which themselves in turn generate others. Out of the Youth Club equipment grants policy came, eventually, such diverse consequences as Endeavour Training on the one hand and clubs for physically handicapped young people on the other. I would not claim that the Trust was directly or even deliberately responsible for these developments. Others had the practical ideas. But they would not have come about unless the Trust, in its empirical one-thing-leads-to-another approach, had not backed an idea – or a person – and made its realisation possible.

One of the fields into which this step-by-step path led was what was then called 'Juvenile Delinquency'. Here the Trust's concern was not so much with bricks and mortar as in financing patient enquiries into the facts and the causes of some rather disquieting phenomena. It was not surprising that some young people, in the tensions and dislocations of the war years, should sometimes behave in ways which their elders found disquieting and disturbing; what was important was to try to find out exactly why they did and what could be done about it. The investigations which the Trust financed were among the earliest, and certainly among the most fruitful, in this complicated field.

In accordance with the Trust's principle of adapting its committee structure to its quinquennial policies I found myself as Convener of a Youth Services Sub-Committee soon after I became a Trustee, then Convener of an Education Sub-Committee after the 'Youth' concern was merged into a wider context, then Convener of a Juvenile Delinquency Sub-Committee when that became a major interest, then again Convener of the Education Sub-Committee when the emphasis on delinquent boys and girls was in turn subsumed under the wider category. Education, as distinct from various supplements to it or deviations from it, was a fairly permanent Trust activity, and I had ten years convening it, until I was made Vice-Chairman of the Trust years later. The Vice-Chairman is elected to serve for five years and then, if he is still alive and *compos mentis*, he succeeds to the Chair. During his vice-chairmanship he has the duty of standing in for any convener who may be unable to attend a quarterly meeting. So, in the natural course of events, he gets an instructively close acquaintance with the activities of each sub-committee, to equip him for the chairmanship which should follow. For various reasons I served not five but ten years as Vice-Chairman until in 1970 I became, in the absence of proved shortcomings, Chairman of the Carnegie United Kingdom Trust.

Meanwhile, there was plenty to do in the world of school. The rule about the chairmanship of the Headmasters' Conference was that after a two-year term you made way for somebody else, with the possibility that you might be elected again after he had done his two years. Hugh Lyon did two years, in 1946 and 1947, and I had two more in 1948 and 1949.

About this time I thought I ought to try to write down something about the public schools. I had what might be thought to be the advantage, from this point of view, of not having been brought up in one myself, so that there was at least the chance of a comparatively fresh and unblinkered eye. The discussions and controversies about the Fleming Report had shown how little was really known about what the schools were really like. Old Boys of them were not always the best expositors. They seemed (and it could be that this is still true) capable of entertaining in their minds simultaneously two mutually contradictory propositions – first, the place is exactly the same as it was when I was there; second, since I left it the place has gone to the dogs. So I tried to describe what the public schools were like as places to live in and work in and grow up in.

It was not easy to do. To begin with, there is no accepted definition of a 'public school'. To most people it means a pretty big and pretty expensive boarding school of some antiquity and independence. But only about one-tenth of the schools whose headmasters are members of the Headmasters' Conference are exclusively boarding schools; one-third of them were founded in the nineteenth century or later; and about one-half of them receive public money in some form or other. It makes for clarity of thought and discussion if these various apparently inextricable strands can be disentangled; but it is difficult to sort out the elements of expense, boarding and independence, with the background thought always in the public mind that this sort of school belongs to, and perpetuates, a privileged minority.

The fundamental difference between the school at which I had been brought up and the schools over which I presided was that it was a day school and they were boarding schools. The advantages and disadvantages of the two species have been, and will continue to be, debated, usually with the generation of more heat than light. For some boys there is no practical alternative, all theories apart, to a boarding school. Their parents work abroad or have jobs which entail frequent changes of residence, and continuity of the children's education almost inevitably demands a boarding school. Then there are the children who have been deprived of one parent, by death or divorce. Again, stability of background makes a boarding school, in many cases at any rate, desirable. But apart from these special categories, why send a boy away from home at the most impressionable stage of his life?

The arguments on both sides are familiar enough, and I have nothing startling to add to them. The boarding school provides a stable and predictable background which some family homes do not; it is a community deliberately designed for the express purpose of helping the development from boyhood to young manhood, which very few ordinary families can be; the numbers and range of ages make possible a variety of acquaintances and shared activities which no family can. On the other hand, to cut a boy off from his own family is, or can be, a serious deprivation; there is, or was, a tendency to make the school an end in itself, to the detriment of the best interests of some of its members; and there could be a deadening monotony, especially for a boy who did not take naturally to routine.

Immense changes have taken place in the boarding schools over the past twenty-five years. They are much more outward-looking, much closer to their local communities, and much less isolated. The degree of compulsoriness, especially in such matters as attendance at Chapel and regulation team-games, is much reduced. The variety of activities, corporate and individual, is greatly increased. Contacts with parents are much closer and more frequent, both for boys and for masters. The rapidly increasing numbers of girls in what had formerly been boys' boarding schools helps to reduce the artificiality of a one-sex establishment.

And there is always the question of money. A boarding school cannot help being an expensive institution, and there must today be thousands of parents who have to ask themselves brutal financial questions which their own parents did not have to face. If you live in London, with a happy family life and intelligent friends whom your children can automatically meet, why spend all that money on sending them to Uppingham or Shrewsbury when you have West-minster and St Paul's and Dulwich on your doorstep? In my own case the problem simply did not arise. My parents could not conceivably have dreamt of finding boarding school fees. If by the waving of some fairy wand I could have gone to Rugby or Repton I wonder what would have happened. I should probably have been miserable socially, at any rate at the start; I could hardly have been better taught than I was at Wakefield; and I might easily have taken on prematurely the outward mask of conformity. So I have no regrets. But I refuse to generalise. Dozens of times people have asked me, 'Which is the best school in the country?' I have always replied: 'There is no such thing as the best school; there is only the best school for a particular boy.'

Inside Shrewsbury School itself one or two problems began to emerge. After the end of the war masters who had been in the forces began to trickle back. They and I were strangers to each other, except for brief calls they might have made when they were on leave. Their jobs were, of course, waiting for them. But some of them had, not surprisingly, been unsettled by their years of different experiences and responsibilities, and not all of them were certain that they wanted to come back. There was the complication that while they had been away other members of the staff had taken on some of the responsibilities of their absent colleagues and in many cases had proved themselves entirely competent to continue. Most difficult of all was the necessity to make some appointments to house-masterships. Several of the most senior men had gone on as house-masters, past the retiring age; they would be glad to be relieved; and their returning colleagues were naturally expecting to succeed them. It was brought sharply home to me one week-end when one of them, not yet released from the Army, straightforwardly asked me which house he was going to have when he came back. I had to tell him, as gently and kindly as I could, that there were several other people in the same position, all of whom would have to be considered, that I had in fact never met him until that morning, and that I could hardly be expected to take the responsibility of promising any house to an almost complete stranger. It all came out in the wash, and I was mercifully able to rely on the good sense and advice of senior colleagues; but it was an awkward can to have to carry.

In general, we had to try to resume a 'normal' school life – which none of the boys then in the School had ever known. Rationing and physical austerity were still with us. But senior boys could begin to look rather further ahead. A new factor came into their lives with the introduction of National Service. Some of them resented this break in their lives, especially those who had hoped to go straight from school to a university. There were all sorts of controversy about the damage to the continuity of their academic careers which would be caused, or the advantage of the added maturity, when they did reach university, which eighteen months of this outside experience would bring. By and large it all worked out sensibly enough, with a considerable degree of flexibility in exemptions and reasonable provision for special cases. Obviously a great deal turned on the particular conditions which individuals were lucky or unlucky enough to encounter. The lucky ones got the chance, for example, of a university-level course in Russian: the unlucky ones square-bashed and skrimshanked with growing disillusion. Some of us felt that the words 'National Service' were being rather narrowly interpreted as service in one of the three armed services, when there was so much civilian work to be done in the restoration of bomb-damage or in catching up on years' worth of inevitable delay in road-building. I did once tentatively suggest to Ernest Bevin that since he was officially Minister of Labour and National Service it might be his Department which allocated these young men to wherever the national needs were greatest, seconding to the services those who were needed there and to civilian occupations those who could be useful there. But I expect there were good reasons why this was not practicable.

Mercifully, life did not consist entirely of re-settlement problems or of national educational policies. One summer day the Head of School came in. If, as he had heard, our elder son had been elected to the top scholarship at Eton, might he be permitted to offer the School's congratulations? Unsuspecting, I made appropriate noises. This being so, sir, might it not be suitable that the School should have a half-holiday to celebrate the fact that, so far as human knowledge went, this was the first time in history that any son of the Headmaster of Shrewsbury had ever done such a thing? At first sight the sheer ingenious effrontery of twisting this happy event into a pretext for a school holiday left me gaping. Then a second thought occurred, that perhaps they really meant that this was a genuinely family celebration. If they did, it would be very ungracious to refuse: if I was being had for a mug, it was in a good cause. So they got their half-holiday. Both the small boy and the suave Head of School became highly competent journalists.

And when, for instance, Uppingham came to play cricket against Shrewsbury and we gave supper to both teams at Kingsland House I was able to leave all twenty-two goggle-eyed by opening the proceedings with the Latin grace used daily in the School House at Uppingham.

Then there was the Rochester Sneath affair. One day in my morning mail was a letter on civilised notepaper from the address of a school in Sussex cordially accepting my invitation to preach in the School Chapel on Sunday, June 10th, and signed, apparently, Rochester Sneath. My secretary was as bewildered as I was. Neither of us was conscious of my having proffered any such invitation, or, indeed, of anybody called Rochester Sneath; and anyway June 10th was booked for somebody else. So I wrote a gentle reply, telling him that unless I had been writing letters in my sleep I had not so invited him, and suggesting that perhaps his letter had been sent to Shrewsbury by mistake for Sherborne. At a meeting of the Committee of the Headmasters' Conference the following week I trotted out this story as an example of what headmasters had to put up with nowadays. The effect was electric. Practically everybody in the room had had a letter from Rochester Sneath. Mine was easily the most innocent. One headmaster had been asked to recommend a London psychiatrist, since it was obvious that in his school there must be a great many psychiatric cases. Another had been told that Rochester Sneath was coming to give away the prizes on his Speech Day and if the headmaster protested all the world would be told what happened on that night in Cairo which he was no doubt anxious to forget. And so on, all round the table. But nobody had a clue who this Rochester Sneath was.

Ten days later my secretary brought in a copy of a weekly magazine containing an article entitled 'Who is Rochester Sneath?' Some enterprising journalist had seen a letter to a newspaper from Rochester Sneath at the school address in Sussex. His was, he wrote, an enterprising new school; he was anxious to introduce the teaching of Russian; could any reader advise him on suitable text-books? The journalist had visited the Sussex village from which the letters ostensibly came. There was no such address as that on the notepaper and neither the village post office nor the village pub knew any gentleman of that name. But the journalist had obviously had access to Rochester Sneath's files, since there were a good many quotations from headmasters' letters, including mine. So the question in the headline remained intriguingly unanswered. Years later, at some worthy meeting in which I was taking part, another participant, whom I had never met before, asked me if the name Rochester Sneath meant anything to me. I said it did, told him why, and asked how he came into it. He said, 'I was Rochester Sneath.' He had been, at the time of the correspondence, a Cambridge undergraduate; he and one of his friends had thought it was quite an entertaining hoax, they had amassed quite a collection of headmasters' autographs, and it had made a good magazine article, hadn't it? His college, I gathered, had taken a different view when the truth came out and had also taken disciplinary measures which seemed to me an unnecessarily harsh reaction to an ingenious and fairly harmless jape.

Then there was 'Tim's'. For many years the School had supported a Mission in Liverpool, and a long line of distinguished School Missioners had made boys from Everton and from Shrewsbury mean something to each other. The parish church of the district where the Mission was, St Timothy's, had taken a real pasting from bombs. It was damaged, dilapidated, and becoming derelict, and with the best will in the world the loyal parishioners simply could not provide enough pairs of hands to do the necessary repairs. Some of us thought that there was a need here, and an opportunity for us to do something practical. After we had worked out plans with local builders, masons, carpenters and hauliers I told the School one morning what we had in mind and asked for volunteers. They must be sixteen or over, because solid physical labour was involved, and they must have the written permission of their parents; numbers would be restricted to ten from each house (School House double) because accommodation was limited and anyway we did not want them tripping over each other, so the total labour force would be limited to a hundred. I gave them a week to think it over, get parental permission and then inform their housemasters. At the end of the week we had twice as many volunteers as places available.

Each week-end a gang went off on Friday night (escaping Saturday morning school) and came back in time for bed on Sunday.

They slept at the Mission, most of them on the floor, and for two solid days they carted bricks, plastered walls, scrubbed the floors, painted pews and generally had one grand and glorious time. Parents and Old Boys in the right lines of business provided free transport, paint, food, bedding. Masters revealed unexpected talents as canteen cooks. The grannies of the parish produced endless cups of tea and expert instruction in floor-scrubbing. Month after month the work went on, with newly-sixteen-year-olds taking the places of eighteen-year-olds who left. Eventually the day came when the Bishop of Liverpool presided at the re-opening of Tim's for public worship, and the most magnificent parish tea ever seen in the history of the diocese was ravenously consumed. The only disappointment expressed was that the job was finished.

I felt that somehow I had never made much impact on Shrewsbury. I do not think that there was any conscious resistance: certainly there was no overt opposition. But Shrewsbury in those days was the kind of school which could to all intents and purposes – or at least to all outward appearance – have got on quite cheerfully without any Headmaster at all. We were very happy, in our lovely house, and so were our children. But there never seemed to be much of what they call a 'challenge'. I like to think it was a happy ship. Certainly a writer in *The Salopian*, as we left, was generous enough to say so. One explanation might be that the place was so settled in its ways that it would never accept that anybody had changed it: another is that it is possible to do good by stealth. The Greeks had a word for it: perhaps Salopians 'escaped their own notice' doing some things slightly differently.

I think this chapter can best end with two quotations. One is from the first letter written to Philip Sidney as a new boy at Shrewsbury by his father, described as the Right Honourable Sir Henry Sidney, Knight of the most Noble order of the Garter, Lord Deputy of Ireland, and Lord President of Wales: 'Be humble and obedient to your master, for unless you frame your self to obey others, yea and feel in your self what obedience is, you shall never be able to teach others how to obey you. Be courteous of gesture, and affable unto all men, with diversity of reverence according to the dignity of the person, there is nothing that winneth so much with so little cost.' The other is from a letter from his mother which is charmingly described in the original as 'in the skirts of my Lord President's letter, to her said son Philip.' 'And for a final leave taking for this time, see that you shew your self as a loving obedient Scholar of your good Master, to govern you yet many years, and that my Lord and I may hear that you profit so in your learning, as thereby you may increase our loving care of you and deserve at his hands the continuance of his great joy, to have him often witness with his own hand the hope he hath in your well doing. Farewell, my little Philip, and once again the Lord bless you.'

Those were the days when letters from parents were worth keeping.

7

Reading University
[1950]

The Vice-Chancellorship of Reading University was an attractive proposition. The University itself was small – by modern standards, tiny – so that I should not be overwhelmed by size or submerged in impersonality. It was very largely residential, so that it was more like the boarding schools I was familiar with than would have been a Redbrick university in a northern industrial town. The composition of its Council, local baronets, members of the Palmer family, representatives of the County and County Borough Education Committees, was similar to governing bodies I had known in schools. It was true that the invitation came at an awkward time. I had had six years at Shrewsbury, and I was in no great hurry to leave. But I had always had at the back of my mind a return to the university world: and in those days, when the number of universities was less than half what it is now, vacancies in vice-chancellorships cropped up very rarely. I was also, to be honest, a bit afraid of getting stuck. I was in my middle forties; I could not, on my proclaimed principles, stay at Shrewsbury for more than another five years, by which time I should be fifty. I did not want to go to a third school; but what else should I be able to do as a fifty-year-old? And if nothing turned up, Shrewsbury would have me round its neck until the retirement bell tolled. So after a pretty thorough reconnaissance of the Reading situation, and a certain amount of swithering, we decided to leave the Severn for the Thames.

The retiring Vice-Chancellor was Sir Frank Stenton, an eminent historian who had spent most of his life at Reading, as devoted to it as he was to his Anglo-Saxons. He had been Vice-Chancellor for only five years, at the end of a scholarly life, and he would have been the last person to claim to be a high-powered administrator or a weighty figure in university politics on the national scale. I suspect he was rather relieved when he reached retiring age and could return to his books.

The University was housed, primarily, in a row of houses on the London Road. Behind the terrace was an attractive little site, with a Library, a Great Hall, covered ways leading from one department to another round a quadrangle of grass, and a War Memorial Clock Tower. Everywhere there were flowers. The Senior Common Room was a former Palmer house, on the edge of the site; it was called *The Acacias*, and there was a magnificent tulip-tree in the middle of the lawn. By comparison with the technological power-house universities of today it was a doll's house; and a very happy one. There was certainly nothing grand about it. The Vice-Chancellor's office was a first-floor converted bedroom, with a pleasant view southwards across the site and plenty of sun. The Registrar was in similar quarters just along the passage, and the Bursar was immediately below. It was all very cosy and entirely unpretentious.

But it was not to stay like that for long. With brilliant imaginative foresight Stenton and the University Council had recently acquired Whiteknights Park, a vast stretch of parkland a mile or so to the south of the London Road buildings. That was what it was, three hundred acres of English parkland with nothing on it but trees, a lake and a few grazing cows. There were just two buildings, big red-brick Victorian mansions, confusingly designated *Park House* and *Whiteknights Park House*. It was suggested that we might live in one or other of them. Stenton, when he became Vice-Chancellor, had gone on living in his own previous farmhouse and his predecessor's Vice-Chancellarial residence had been taken over as an annexe to a women's hall of residence. So there was no settled abode for a new Vice-Chancellor and if he opted for one of the two white elephants in Whiteknights Park that would solve two of the University's problems at one stroke – what to do with the new Vice-Chancellor and what to do with one of these two horrors. At the end of a hot and tiring afternoon the prospective Vice-Chancellor and his wife agreed, by the mutual lifting of eyebrows and the exchange of other arcane signs, that they would have nothing to do with either. They were obviously too big – one later became the temporary home of Reading's renowned Museum of English Rural

Life, and the other became a hall of residence for thirty men – but, much worse, each of them was a full quarter of a mile from the nearest bus stop. And those four hundred yards were along an ill-lit footpath through an uninhabited piece of open parkland. How could one possibly acquire, still less keep, any domestic staff? Eventually, these two having been flatly turned down, we went to live in what was easily the most ugly and much the most convenient of the many tied cottages we have inhabited. It was a simple oblong two-storey brick box, built about 1910, with no cellars and no attics, but with the necessary number of small bedrooms for a growing-up family and a splendid drawing-room across the width of the house which had its uses for staff parties – and for children's parties too. The acre of garden had been admirably planned; and it too did its share at parties. There was a bit of difficulty in ejecting the sitting tenants; but the name of Palmer had its weight, and why not, since it had been built to house a widowed Palmer fifty years before?

But these were comparatively trivial domestic details – like the spotted flycatchers who sat on our telephone wires and nested, year after year, in the Virginia creeper which covered the front of the house. The development of the Whiteknights Park site was to be the first concern of the new Vice-Chancellor. This was quite a problem. Given a virgin site of that size, how do you begin to plan its development for a small but growing university? How far can you envisage a final design when you do not know how firmly you can rely on money to realise it? Do you begin with halls of residence or with dazzling departmental buildings to house computers or other bits of magic? How far do you conform to the existing contours of undulation and lake, or how far do you bulldoze all that into what will be most 'cost-effective'? We were abundantly fortunate from the start in two personalities. The chairman of the committee charged with the development of the Park was Gerald Palmer. He and I did not always agree about everything; so, naturally, I did not always think that he was right. But he knew about land and trees and buildings, and he could contribute what I as the brash upstart academic could not contribute to the conversion of a great stretch of English parkland to a quite different use. We had our disagreements: but it may be that the outcome of our differences of opinion was more fruitful than if we had been in tepid agreement from the start.

The other considerable personality involved in all this was our architect, Howard Robertson. He was the senior partner in the firm to which the University entrusted the development of the site. Other partners were, of course, involved, notably Leslie Preston. But the strategy of the whole affair was Robertson's. And I have never, before or since, come across a more deliberately modest or self-effacing approach in any architect. Our first building on the new site was to be a new building for the Faculty of Letters; so there were no preconceptions about being 'with it', still less 'way out', as might have been the case if we had been talking about buildings for science or technology. I shall always remember a long and 'back-hair-down' conversation. I recognised the opportunity and the challenge which this new site for a growing university presented. He could not help being professionally thrilled at the opportunity to do what he blank-well pleased with such a marvellous piece of untouched parkland. But, it soon became clear, he had a conscience, not only professional but historical. Whatever he did now, the chances were that the total development of the site would take twenty years, and by the end of that time how would his 1950-ish ideas look? It was not for him, by the design of this first building, to cramp, still less to determine, the style of his successors; they must have the freedom which he was fortunate enough to enjoy at the very birth of the development. So he deliberately designed the Faculty of Letters building not in a dashing distinctive 'individualistic' style which would prejudge the nature of the buildings on the site for ever after, but in a self-chosen low-key college-cottage-Gothic idiom which left his successors free to move outwards from there in whatever direction they should choose. If anybody should ever call that first building on Whiteknights Park 'undistinguished' they should appreciate that it was quite deliberately planned to be unregulative of the future. Not many great architects would have been as modest as that.

More important, from my point of view, than bricks and mortar, were my relations with colleagues and students. So far as the former were concerned, there had been, as some of them let out years afterwards, some suspicions about 'this headmaster' and his likely manner of behaviour. In a way it was not unlike what Shrewsbury had feared on my arrival from Uppingham. What the Reading community perhaps did not at first wholly grasp was that before I had ever been a headmaster I had been a member of the democratic academic fraternity of an Oxford college, and that the accidentally authoritarian attributes of a headmaster were genuinely accidental and not so ingrained that they could not be shed. It was not all that difficult to preside at meetings of the Senate, in a Speaker-like way, for somebody who had seen George Gordon presiding at a College Meeting. Indeed, the two bodies were not very dissimilar. It must be difficult for those who are familiar only with the swollen senates in universities today to believe that the Senate at Reading in my early days was in actual numbers no bigger than the College Meetings I had known at Magdalen. We were thirty-odd, arranged round a hollow square of tables, so that there could be real debate, with assertion and counter-assertion. (We also had the civilised habit of meeting at five o'clock, so that for obvious reasons no Senate could last for more than two hours.) We did not meet, as the modern habit seems to be, in a semi-circular chamber, where one member after another rises to read aloud page after page of typescript prepared by his secretary. There was plenty of cut and thrust, but it was all conducted with decorum – gowns and no smoking – and a degree of formality which did not inhibit plain speaking. Here again I was very fortunate in my senior colleagues. Many of them had been there for many years, preferring the friendliness of comparatively small departments to the ambitious bustle of bigger universities. My most sagacious mentor was the Registrar, Ernest Smith, whose connection with the place went back to its University College days before the Royal Charter of 1926. There was nothing he did not know about its history or its personalities; quiet, hesitant of speech, pellucidly honest, totally trusted by everybody, and entirely without personal ambition, he was also as shrewd and acute as they come.

He perhaps had a clearer picture than anybody else of the changes that were facing us. There was a general air of restlessness throughout the universities. They were trying to resume a normal life after the upheavals of the war years. So were the schools. But whereas most of these had been able, in spite of evacuations and scatterings, to keep their normal flow of boys coming and going, that was not so with the universities. Their undergraduate numbers had been reduced to the medically unfit, the exempted categories and those girls who for one reason or another were still civilians. Buildings had been requisitioned; whole departments had been diverted from normal teaching and research to projects of immediate national importance. Essentially there was a backlog of five years' intakes to cope with, on top of a resumption of the natural flow from the schools. So there was urgent need for drastic expansion. Physically, we at Reading were luckier than most, with the whole of White-knights Park to expand into. But you cannot plan and build a new university overnight. For one thing, you have to decide on your academic strategy before you can plan the buildings to match it.

Some of my colleagues were disturbed by the sheer magnitude of what was contemplated. Hour after hour of debate went on, in Senate, in faculty boards and in planning committees. Remember, Reading had always been an intimate, unpretentious and domestic society, and there were many who wanted to keep it so. In retrospect the watershed was when the momentous decision was taken, laughable as it must now seem, to increase student numbers up to 1,200. That, of course, meant a corresponding increase in the size of the academic staff, and the consequence of that would be, as somebody plaintively protested, 'But, Vice-Chancellor, that will mean that there will be people coming in to Senior Common Room whom we don't know by sight.' But it was either that or stagnation, and the Council, expertly handled by Sir George Mowbray, deeply experienced in public affairs, was emphatically not in favour of stagnation.

Eventually the great day came when work was actually to begin on the first building in Whiteknights Park. There had, inevitably, been delays. By monstrous mischance the boundary between the County Borough of Reading and the County of Berkshire ran slap through the middle of the site, so there were two separate planning authorities to consult; and although both were entirely benevolent and helpful it all took time. Building materials were scarce, and so was labour. But with triumph and some ceremony we were ready to cut the first sod or turn the first turf, in the middle of what was then an open field. It was universally agreed that this should be Stenton's privilege, as the *fons et origo* of the whole affair. So he was armed with a spade almost as big as himself and he dexterously removed the previously-loosened turf. Shouldering the spade, he began a superb speech with the epic words, 'Unaccustomed, er, as I, er, am to, er, public digging ...' One advantage of having so much space was that we could put the buildings where they would not interfere with the park's magnificent trees.

Relations with students were almost unalloyed bliss. I suppose that of all the changes which have come over the universities in the past twenty years no single one has been more poignant than the change in relationships between the student body and 'the University authorities'. Obviously, there are places and times nowadays where these are pleasant and friendly, and where there is mutual confidence and goodwill. Twenty years ago it never crossed anybody's mind that there would be anything else. When I read about the rifling of a vice-chancellor's private files, or obscenities shouted at him as he goes about his unassuming business, or bricks thrown through the windows of his house, I realise how lucky I was to be in that job when I was; and I sometimes think that anybody who contemplates taking it on nowadays ought to have his head examined. Of course there were occasional bits of tiresomeness; what else can you expect if you have a thousand healthy and high-spirited youngsters living at close quarters with each other? Now and then a bunch of men would invade a women's hall of residence and throw a girl into a bath. (It was sometimes not unreasonably suspected that there might have been provocation.) Now and then a publican from a village in the Cotswolds had pungent comment to make to the Vice-Chancellor on the behaviour of a football XV on its way back from a match. (As if that had never happened before.) And just once or twice the magazine produced in connection with Rag Week came in for criticism from the local clergy (though greatly appreciated by the townsfolk who bought it). But compared with recent years the recollection is of almost unbelievably Garden-of-Eden innocence. It was, heaven knows, not because they were cowed or down-trodden or spiritless; they certainly were none of these things. They just seemed, bless them, to have more sense than some of their successors. They had a proper degree of ordinary naughtiness; but I could count on the fingers of one hand the really wounding cases that occurred in thirteen years. And for once I am prepared to sound as *laudator temporis acti* as you like.

I think this was partly due to the fact that the University was largely residential. Whatever anybody says I remain an unashamed advocate of the civilising and humanising influences of residential life in a university. In those old-fashioned days there were separate halls of residence for men and for women, and nobody, to my recollection, ever wanted anything different. When the possibility of mixed halls was mentioned the general reaction was, 'Heavens, can't I go to the loo in my pyjamas without the risk of meeting a girl in the corridor?' Or, 'But if I go around at night with my hair in curlers do I have to run the risk of bawdy greetings from anybody I meet?' Plainly, a great deal depended (as it always does) on the common sense and sensitivity of the wardens, male and female; and we were very lucky indeed at that time. They did not always agree *inter se* at wardens' meetings; some were more rigorous and some more permissive, and once or twice there had to be reminders that there were University rules which must be observed, whatever local by-laws there might be in this hall or that. I suppose that this whole approach would nowadays be regarded as ludicrously paternalistic. I made no secret of my view that we did in some sense stand *in loco parentis*, that we had a responsibility to the parents of a boy or girl from a village in Somerset, living away from home for the first time in their lives, and, indeed, a responsibility to the youngsters themselves. All I can say is that they seemed to thrive on it; they enjoyed themselves; they behaved (usually) as responsible members of a society; and I believe they genuinely meant it when they said that they were glad that they were there.

The other important factor was the presence of a high proportion of young women. It was about two girls to three men, and, as one of the minority once said to me at a dance, 'Well, you've got to write off one man in three anyway, so that makes it virtually all square.' I have no doubt that this sort of numerical equality made for civilised living. The rules of the Students' Union required that of whichever sex the President of the Union was the Senior Vice-President should be of the other. In my time the President was almost always a man, because in those days the women were not as 'politically conscious' as they are now; but one of the best Presidents we ever had was a woman.

It was an accepted practice that the President of the Union dropped in on me every day, at some time or other when we both happened to be free. Usually there was nothing in particular to talk about; but generations of Presidents consumed my sherry and cigarettes without our necessarily having issues of great moment to discuss. Simply, there was a daily opportunity for either of us to mention casually whatever he might wish to raise, in the context of a low-relief routine. This was long before the days when Union Presidents had what is inaccurately called a 'sabbatical year' to devote themselves to their full-time political occupations. I warned each President-elect, when he was first brought to see me after his election, that this would probably cost him one Class in his Final Honours but might well increase his chances of a job with Shell. One confounded me, and all subsequent theorisers, by being President in his last year as an undergraduate and getting a First; but he had done his National Service in the Navy and there learnt how to organise his time. He it was also who appeared at my door one morning as usual, but this time hand in hand with a girl who was President of her hall Junior Common Room. 'Oh,' said I, 'at last. I've been expecting this for months. I take it, from the silly simper on your faces, that you are now engaged.' 'No,' said he, firmly advancing into the room with fingers still intertwined, 'lots of people get engaged: we are engaged to be married – that's quite different.'

Rather unexpectedly I acquired a Nigerian godson. A young Nigerian had come to do postgraduate research in the Department of Agricultural Botany, bringing with him a wife who was doing a teacher's diploma in the Department of Education. Their first-born arrived and the father came to see me, in attractive embarrassment. 'Sir, we have in this country two families, our Church and our University. One of the ladies of our Church has consented to be godmother to our child; is it possible that you might be his god-father?' I said of course I would. It was a marvellous christening, one Sunday afternoon in a tin-roofed church on the outskirts of Reading. All their Nigerian friends from the whole of Britain came, some in snappy Western clothes, some in full Nigerian dress. And this one jet-black child was baptised with three other conspicuously white ones, he in the same ritual clothes as they, white cap, knitted white gloves, the lot. At the reception in the Church Hall afterwards somebody found a gramophone and some records, and as the afternoon became evening and then night Olu's baptism was properly celebrated with a gloriously ecumenical festival of dance.

One serious deprivation was that I was not able to do any teaching. There was no statutory ban. But it would obviously be awkward for the Professor of Philosophy to have a maverick Vice-Chancellor loose in his department; and for understandable reasons the Vice-Chancellor could not guarantee regular and punctual attendance at departmental engagements. I did later on get an invitation, which I grabbed with both hands. A new and enterprising young Professor of Agricultural Botany, after he had surveyed his bailiwick for a couple of years, said to me one day, 'I suppose, Vice-Chancellor, you wouldn't like to come and do a sort of seminar with my final-year Honours students?' I told him that what I knew about agricultural botany would not cover a sixpence. 'Oh, I know that,' he replied, 'that was not my idea at all. What I had in mind was something quite different. I am appalled by what I regard as the shocking ignorance of these youngsters about the fundamentals. They seem to have no idea of the concepts of proof or hypothesis or what makes a statement true or false. They won't take it from me, because I am an agricultural botanist; and I don't want to bother my colleagues in the Philosophy Department, because they have enough on their plates already. I'm not suggesting that you haven't. But if you could spare the time to come over just once or twice and twist their mental tails a bit I am sure it would do us all good.' It developed into a fortnightly session throughout the term, with the staff of the Department present as well, repeated annually until I had to withdraw because of other pressures. While it lasted it was quite like old times. But I would not have believed, when I left Oxford, that my next university teaching assignment would be in a Department of Agricultural Botany.

There were two forms of public activity which were new to me but which seemed to be part of the job. One was giving away prizes at schools. It was thought to be a good thing that the Vice-Chancellor should do this, as a public relations exercise or a 'contribution to closer integration' or just plain waving of the Reading flag. It sometimes seemed to me that there was a risk that all this effort might be counter-productive, but I dutifully did it. And I am prepared to make a small bet that I have given away prizes at more schools in England than any other ex-don, ex-headmaster or ex-vice-chancellor. Middle-aged men at City dinners or elegant young wives at cocktail parties are constantly saying, 'Oh, the last time we met – but you won't remember – was when you came and gave away the prizes at my school.' And, of course, I have to ask them where that was and pretend to remember. Almost invariably they were enjoyable occasions. But thirty-five mortal minutes of handing out GCE certificates, plus another twenty minutes' worth of prizes for every conceivable subject (and some hardly conceivable ones) begin to induce a backache which leaves the distinguished visitor at something less than his best when having done all that he has to utter words which the local Press will report as it, rather than he, chooses.

One of the schools I visited for this purpose was Benenden, where Princess Anne was in her second year. I had in fact done the job there before, but a new Headmistress invited me again, so that ever since I have been able to claim Benenden and bar. On the afternoon of Speech Day there was an outdoor presentation of the Pageant of Benenden House. Episodes from its history were narrated and then enacted, while the assembled parentry sat on the terrace and watched. Suddenly, on the opposite side of the valley, a slim figure was seen thundering downhill on a horse, aiming, at top speed, for a narrow gap in the wall at the bottom of a field. All the girls of the school knew this to be Princess Anne, and there were 'Oohs' and 'Ahs' from them and their parents at the apparent recklessness of the rider. The Queen turned round in her deck-chair and said, with a smile of total calm, 'You needn't worry – if there's one thing the child can do it's ride a horse.' Seconds later a flushed young girl, in period dress and high boots, flung herself from her panting horse, and presented herself as the messenger sent on ahead to announce the impending arrival at Benenden House of Queen Elizabeth the First. A pretty piece of casting – and of performance.

The other new ploy was participation in local affairs. And here, since Reading was the administrative capital of Berkshire as well as being a County Borough, there was a double obligation. I sat on the two Education Committees, of Berkshire and of Reading, and on their Higher Education Sub-Committees. I became Chairman of the Governors of Reading School; and that was an illuminating experience. Reading School was an unusual institution in that its history went back to the days of Reading Abbey, it numbered Archbishop Laud among its old boys, and it was now a maintained school in a County Borough with, uniquely, a hundred boarders. Its record in University scholarships was consistently high; but I felt it my conscientious duty to advise that its day-boys should go to some university other than the local one. I am not sure that it is a good thing for ex-headmasters to be chairmen of governing bodies of schools. But I hope I never forgot the dictum of Claude Blagden, whom you may remember as Chairman of the Uppingham governing body when I first became a headmaster, that it would be unseemly for either of us to try to do the other's job.

I took no part in local party politics. I do not believe that headmasters or vice-chancellors should. Reading County Borough was at that time very delicately balanced between the two major parties, and at each new round of municipal elections the scale might be turned by the result in one or two wards. Once, and only once, did I intervene in local politics, towards the end of my time there. At the recent elections the Labour Party had acquired a paper-thin majority of councillors. But with aldermen counted in they were in a paper-thin minority. They announced their intention of filling all the forthcoming aldermanic vacancies with nominees of their own party, to ensure their overall majority in the Council. There were hot protests from the Tories. Feeling in the town ran, as they say, high. The local newspapers rang with protest and counter-protest. Personal friendships were shattered, and X was no longer on speaking terms with Y. I heard both sides, from individuals who were deeply involved, Tories saying how monstrous a perversion of democracy this was, Labour replying that the Tories had started it by doing exactly the same when they had a very small majority of councillors. It seemed to me that whatever the rights and wrongs might be the whole atmosphere of public life in Reading was being poisoned, and I felt that as a total non-partisan perhaps I ought to do something about it, simply to try to restore civic health and decent friendliness between fellow citizens. The Mayor at the time had been a Labour councillor, himself a most successful example of the success of private enterprise in his own business, and scrupulous about his non-party position as Mayor. I rang him up at his home one Sunday morning and asked if I might come and see him. 'Sure, come now.' So I got in my car and went. He met me with a drink and the words 'I know why you've come.' I began to explain. He told me there was no need, he entirely understood my unprecedented intervention. I asked if there was anything I could do. Would the party leaders meet privately under my obviously impartial roof and at least arrive at some sort of joint statement which I could publish? The Mayor asked if I would go and see the leader of the Conservatives and make that proposition to him. I said

No: I was talking to him as Mayor, not as a Labour leader. He revealed that the Party caucus was meeting that evening; he was going to be present; he personally agreed with my view that the aldermanic vacancies should be filled proportionately to the party numbers of councillors; he would tell them so, and tell them that I had put this view to him; and he would ring me up when the meeting was over to let me know the outcome. I waited up until long after midnight, but no message came. He rang next morning. The meeting had gone on until three o'clock; but, he was glad to say, common sense had eventually prevailed and the vacancies would be filled proportionately.

Then there were the monthly meetings of the Vice-Chancellors' Committee. In those days it was not the active policy-making body which, in greatly changed circumstances, it has since become. It was much more like a luncheon-club, with some discussion of matters of common interest, but with no decisions or adoptions of a 'party line'. Indeed, anybody who spoke was at pains to say that he could not, of course, express the view of his university, that was for his council and senate to determine, but if the Committee thought it necessary he would seek to ascertain that view on his return. Some of the 'new-style' vice-chancellors, ex-headmasters or ex-diplomats rather than ex-professors, regarded this as all rather feeble, futile and frustrating. I attended pretty regularly, simply to learn and to get the feel of things. Nowadays, of course, the Committee of Vice-Chancellors and Principals, with its enormously increased membership, is a powerful force in presenting to the Government, to the public and to students a corporate view on behalf of the universities as a body. This must be much more difficult now, when its membership is so much bigger and so much less homogenous, than it would have been then; and it says much for the statesmanship and political skill of successive chairmen that the C V C P carries the weight and authority it nowadays does.

Meanwhile, there were calls from the outside world. I quickly became aware that Reading was dangerously near to London, and its Vice-Chancellor therefore particularly vulnerable for committees of every kind. The first major one was the Secondary School Examinations Council. It had been felt for some time that the various School Certificate and Higher Certificate examinations conducted by various university boards were rather an untidy mess. Nobody –

or practically nobody – wanted to see a great national centralisation on the continental pattern. But reasonable comparability of standards would be a good thing, and so would some guarantee of reciprocity in university entrance requirements. More important than that, it was widely felt that as they stood these examinations imposed an intolerable inflexibility on the schools, whose curricula and teaching practices were largely determined by the needs of the minority who intended to go to university. Further, there were now to be taken into account boys and girls who were not at grammar schools but ought to have the chance of acquiring qualifications with an accepted currency. So altogether there was an accumulated mass of reasons why the whole business of external examinations in secondary schools should be looked at. Before I took over Philip Morris had broken the back of it and my five years in the chair were mainly concerned with sorting out the practical details of 'A' level and 'O' level, with selling the proposals to the schools and the universities, and to the inauguration of two new examining bodies for the purpose of taking off some of the existing boards what seemed excessive loads. Notions which seemed revolutionary then have come to be taken for granted by now, and in some cases discarded as obsolete.

A quite different area of activity was the National Council of Social Service. I have never known how I came to be landed with this particular task. Perhaps the then incumbent, Keith Murray, on his translation to the Chairmanship of the University Grants Committee, thought that the Vice-Chancellor of Reading had nothing much to do and could easily take the National Council of Social Service in his stride. I simply do not know. I do know that the NCSS has given to at least one vice-chancellor an interest and a concern which have lasted to the present day, and a dimension to his public activities which not every vice-chancellor has been fortunate enough to enjoy. At the meetings of the Council and its Executive Committee there was never a dull moment. In the circumstances of today there may well be debate about the precise nature and function of 'the voluntary principle' and of its relation to statutory authorities of one kind or another. That is not a topic for discussion here. What is clear, to me at any rate, is that if voluntary activity has a place in our society – and I deeply feel that it has – then it is essential that the NCSS or some similar body should be its mouthpiece.

Meanwhile, building operations were going on in Whiteknights Park, with all the usual delays and frustrations. There was a big day when I climbed a ladder and set foot on the skeleton of a first floor in the Faculty of Letters Building. But the biggest day of all came in March of 1957, when Her Majesty the Queen, accompanied by Prince Philip, graciously visited us and officially opened this first of the many buildings which have since then transformed a piece of open parkland into a humming university campus.

In the course of the afternoon there were three unexpected items, two at least of which I ought to have had the gumption to foresee. The first, actually, I had – to some extent but not wholly. Discussing the arrangements in advance with Michael Adeane, The Queen's Private Secretary, I had proposed that Her Majesty should turn a key in the lock of the new building and enter. This, I found, was unacceptable. There was the traumatic recollection of the occasion when King George VI had turned a key in the lock of the New Bodleian Building at Oxford and the lock had obstinately refused to obey, so that somebody had had to race round inside and open the thing: since then royal key-turnings were off. I protested that I did not regard the cutting of a bit of ribbon as adequate: it was a building we were opening, not a road or a bridge or a housing estate, and if you were opening a building how could you do it except by turning a key in a lock and opening the door? After prolonged (and entirely amicable) argument I promised that, so help me God, the key would turn in the lock; and under threat of imprisonment in the Tower if I failed this was eventually accepted. I went back to the architect with the simple proposition that we should de-gut the lock, so that there was in fact nothing for the key to do. He was horrified: he had laid on the best locksmiths in England and how could he make their devoted work nugatory in this way? I insisted. And so it was. Her Majesty turned the key, the door was opened, and the procession entered. I ventured to ask if she had found any difficulty in making the lock work. None. So I explained what I had organised, and why. Prince Philip, with his characteristic determination to find out how things work, overhearing the explanation, went back across the lobby, peered deeply into the lock and returned to report that, as I had said, the lock had no innards.

The second item was due to my lack of foresight. If you are leading a procession with The Queen and you suddenly see in front of you a pair of swing doors which meet in the middle, what do you do? I shoved like anything on the inner hinge, and Her Majesty gracefully slipped through – but only just. Two minutes later the same problem recurred, and I simply could not expect The Queen to duck under my arm again. So I boldly marched through and held it open, cursing myself for not having had the wit to lay on somebody to fling it open with a flourish.

The third occurred during tea, when Her Majesty was receiving, as I bowled them up, professors, girl students from the West Indies, Presidents of hall Junior Common Rooms, each for three minutes. She suddenly broke off, in the middle of one conversation, and said to me, 'Oh, by the way, what did you think of that banner?' 'Banner, Ma'am, what banner?' 'You know, the banner down the side of the building.' 'I'm sorry, Ma'am, I didn't know that there was a banner. What does it say?' 'Oh no, if you don't know it's there, I'm not going to tell you what it says. I'll tell you this, it's nothing you need worry about.' So, in spite of further protests, I had to wait, teased by a delicious sense of mischief which not everybody associates with Her Majesty. I pleaded that if I was not told we should all have to rush out after the Royal departure to see what the banner did say. Unbeknown to me, a bunch of the young from our School of Fine Art had secreted themselves on the roof of the new building, and as the Royal party approached had unfurled a huge banner, inscribed, in cockeyed Art School capitals, with the blazon WELCOME TO THE HOUSE THAT JACK BUILT. On the morning of that same day we had held a domestic ceremony to confer honorary doctorates on the three persons mainly responsible, Gerald Palmer, Chairman of the Building Committee, Howard Robertson, the architect, and Ernest Smith, the Registrar.

During this same year an entirely new interest came our way, which has continued and deepened year by year down to the present. A letter came from Maurice Bowra, asking if my wife and I would care to join the team of guest-lecturers which accompanied the Hellenic Cruises organised by Swan's in conjunction with the Hellenic Travellers' Club. My wife's father and mother had in fact been on such cruises many years ago, when they were much less well known and much more primitive. Then the travellers were almost all dons or schoolmasters or undergraduates. Now, under new management, they were becoming increasingly well known as providing a holiday with a purpose to it; and to enable the passengers to get the most out of it a small band of expert lecturers accompanied each cruise. My only misgiving was that I was not an expert, never having been a professional archaeologist or ancient historian. Such hesitations were swept down the wind of a Bowra boom; and we went, for the first of countless times. The number of cruises arranged each year has steadily grown, and a succession of more or less stately ships has carried more and more Hellenic Travellers round the Aegean.

The function of the lecturers on these journeys is an interesting one. They are not guides to the sites visited; that detailed job is done by four or five extremely competent Greeks who really do know their stuff and are, besides, very intelligent and charming companions. The lecturers are supposed to do the more 'broad-brush' background introductions, and to be available for general conversation with the passengers. These last present a marvellously assorted company – dons, Cabinet ministers, ambassadors, American widows, Birmingham businessmen, retired hospital matrons, and, mercifully, a healthy sprinkling of male and female undergraduates who sleep in dormitories and keep the lecturers on their toes. It is hard work, for the passengers, as well as for the 'staff', because there are plenty of early-morning starts and plenty of hills to climb; some have been heard to whisper that they will have to have a holiday when they get back, to recover. For our part, we have made a multitude of friends, Greek, British, American, some of whom are now among our closest and dearest; we have visited places we could never conceivably have reached on our own; we have accumulated an endless collection of good stories, about Maurice Bowra, Mortimer Wheeler, Ian Richmond, and many others; and we have heard Harold Macmillan reciting Aeschylus in Greek in the theatre of Dionysus in Athens.

When I first went to Reading the Chancellor of the University was Lord Templewood. It is not my business to have a view about Sir Samuel Hoare as a Foreign Secretary. I can only say that as Chancellor of a university Lord Templewood was impeccable. He had a clear doctrine about a Chancellor's duty. He was there to make occasional ceremonial appearances (which he did very well), to give whatever help he could whenever the Vice-Chancellor might ask for it (but not unless), and otherwise to keep out of everybody's hair (which he did with dignity and skill). He gave me generously of his time and experience whenever I asked for it – often about whether I should or should not take on this job or that. We had not been at Reading more than a couple of years when I was invited by the then Secretary of State for Commonwealth Relations to go as High Commissioner to one of the major Commonwealth countries. This really did cause some heart-searching. It was a job of a magnitude and importance far beyond anything I had so far attempted. It might lead to all sorts of other things. But it would mean a complete switch to an entirely different kind of career, with an unpredictable future. The children were at difficult ages either to leave or to take with us. But, most importantly, was it fair to the University to create a situation in which it would have had three different Vice-Chancellors in four years? Sam Templewood was a rock through all the discussions and debates. In the end, after what the Secretary of State must have thought inexcusable vacillation, the answer was 'No'. Looking back, it is fascinating to indulge in 'What if' speculations. If the answer had been 'Yes', that certainly would have been a turning point.

In 1959 Templewood died, having been Chancellor for twenty-two years, and it was necessary to take the appropriate steps to find a successor. He had been in office for so long that nobody could quite remember what those steps were. But it seemed pretty safe to appoint a joint committee of Council and Senate and to ask the Vice-Chancellor to prepare a memorandum. Doing this involved making explicit and fairly specific what the function and duties of a Chancellor should be. I recited all the obvious ones, and inserted one which perhaps was not so obvious, that in the event of a real crisis in the University's affairs he should be able to lift his telephone and speak to the Chancellor of the Exchequer, whatever Party was in power, on Christian-name terms. This narrowed the field not a little. When I was challenged with the question whether I had drawn up this job-specification with any one person particularly in mind, I cheerfully acknowledged, 'Yes, of course: Edward Bridges.' He had lately retired from the monumental tripartite role of Secretary to the Cabinet, Permanent Secretary to the Treasury and Head of the Civil Service. There was nothing he did not know about Whitehall and the machinery of government. He was the son of a Poet Laureate, he had been academically distinguished at Eton and

Magdalen, and he was, essentially, a wise old bird. I had encountered him, you may remember, at breakfast in the United University Club during 1941; and it seemed possible that if he were asked he might take us on. He was, and he did, to the immense advantage of the University and the personal pleasure of all who came to know him.

If the procedures for appointing a Chancellor were rather obscure, the manner of actually installing him was so far buried in the past that nobody had a clue. So he and I made it up for ourselves. We had hilarious rehearsals, marching about my room reciting our words in the presence of tolerantly amused wives, he, as his custom was, thumping me hard in the chest every time our paths crossed. I required that he should be kept waiting outside the Great Hall until he was summoned. I further required the Professor of Music to produce a fanfare for the Chancellor's entrance. He pleaded that he had composed one for The Queen two years ago; could we not use that again? I insisted that we could not conceivably greet the Chancellor with a second-hand fanfare, even though it be in origin a Royal one. Very well then, how long a fanfare did we need? I took the Head Porter, who would be leading the procession; we paced out the distance from my room to the door of the Great Hall; and I told the Professor of Music that we should need thirty-five yards of fanfare. It was duly composed, *de novo*, Edward waiting until he was summoned; he was escorted, in solemn silence, from the door to the dais; he was required to pledge himself to uphold the Statutes and Ordinances of the University; and I thereupon admitted him, vacating to him the central throne and taking a humbler chair at his shoulder for the Honorary Degree ceremony which followed his installation and his inaugural speech. He became a close family friend, as well as a superb Chancellor. His unsophisticated humour and deep wisdom, his personal gaiety and his sense of occasion, made me well content that I had deliberately fudged the job-specification.

All this time student numbers were growing at what seemed fantastic speed. By 1959 we had reached nearly 1,500; and if that sounds minute by present-day standards it was almost a fifty-per-cent increase during my few years there. We planned to touch 2,000 by 1965, doubling the population within five undergraduate generations. Academic developments, naturally, had to keep pace with numerical growth. We widened the range of what the Americans charmingly call our 'offerings'; new departments came into existence by the process known as 'hiving-off'; greatly increased numbers of postgraduate students came to us from all over the world. Reading's reputation had originally been based on its agricultural studies, and that reputation continued to be fully maintained by the Faculty of Agriculture and Horticulture. But now we were developing a broader base, right across from Sedimentology to Italian and from Physiological Psychology to Landscape Architecture. New buildings, inevitably, were not always forthcoming when they were wanted. The University Grants Committee did their best for us, and treated us very generously; but there was simply not enough money to go round when everybody else was doing just what we were but on a bigger scale. However, by 1963 we had in Whiteknights Park, besides the Faculty of Letters Building, a Department of Physics, a Research Laboratory in Sedimentology and, our real pride and joy, a new Library, admirably designed by Leslie Preston. And there were two new halls of residence, besides considerable extensions to others.

When I left, the University generously gave me my first Honorary Doctorate. The County Borough also went on record with a very cordial resolution of appreciation and thanks. More, they had it beautifully engrossed on vellum, sealed with their ancient seal, and embedded in slate. More still, the Town Clerk ingeniously discovered illustrations to decorate the margins: the coats of arms of Wakefield Grammar School, Queen's, the Air Training Corps, Reading University; crossed hockey sticks, an Athenian warrior, a microphone – and one other object, which puzzled many until they realised that it was a vice, no doubt in punning allusion to the operation recorded in Chapter 8 of this book.

8

The Committee on Homosexual
Offences and Prostitution
[1954]

The telephone call from the Home Secretary's Private Office on that summer morning in 1954 was entirely unexpected. Could I make it convenient to call on the Home Secretary sometime within the next few days? There was no immediate hurry. It was about a new committee he had in mind to set up; he would tell me all about it himself. Yes, next Tuesday would do perfectly well.

By chance I had to be in Liverpool on the intervening Friday, returning to London by the sleeper train. Inquisitively looking down the list of fellow travellers, as one always does, I was entertained to find the name of Sir David Maxwell Fyfe, the Home Secretary, who had presumably been on a visit to his constituency. As the train left I wrote a note suggesting that if it would save his time next week we might have some conversation now. His detective took it in to him and came back with the reply that the Home Secretary would be very glad to see me straight away.

I suspect that he had been half undressed when he got my message. But he nobly put his overcoat over what was left; and so it happened that my first conversation about this whole business took place as we sat side by side on his sleeping-berth. By the time I left him after Crewe and lurched back to my own compartment my head was in a fair whirl. I was still to call on him the following Tuesday, to meet the Permanent Secretary and, obviously, to have my arm twisted.

The situation, as outlined then and further expounded the following week, was this. The Home Office had a wide and rather ill-defined responsibility in the field of relationships between individual citizens and the law. On the one hand was a proper regard for civil liberties: on the other was the duty to preserve law and order. Sometimes the balance of emphasis would swing one way, sometimes the other. Freedom within the law was the watch-word; but it was not always easy to reconcile the freedoms of everybody concerned. And when it came to the enforcement of the law the police were inevitably involved and then a more direct responsibility fell on the Home Office.

Against that broad-brush background the Home Secretary had two specific worries, and they were both in the highly sensitive realm of sexual behaviour. This was always a particularly delicate area, because issues of morality were involved besides questions of legality; and at a time when traditional standards of morality were being questioned or abandoned there was a general atmosphere of unsettlement and increasing indecision. The two specific problems were prostitution and homosexual behaviour between men; the reasons for his disquiet were different in the two cases, but they were both worrying.

In relation to the former, there was increasing public concern at what was regarded as the growing shamelessness of prostitutes in the streets of London and some other big cities. Granted that prostitution was not in itself an offence against the law, soliciting was, and it was becoming more open and more persistent. Besides breaking the law, they were, by flaunting themselves and pestering passers-by, causing an intolerable degree of embarrassment and giving to visitors a deplorable impression of London's immorality. Each had her own pitch; trespassing led to altercation and violence; and innocent young women waiting for friends had been beaten up. There were suspicions also that the law was being brought into disrepute. It was hinted that in the West End of London the police operated on a rota, pulling in the girls once every so often in turn. They then appeared in court and were fined the nugatory amounts the law allowed, recouping themselves in the course of business for what were regarded as normal overhead expenses of the trade. It was not very clear what could be done about all this, but, questions of morality apart, something must be, in protection of the right of the ordinary citizen to have free and uninterrupted passage along the streets of the capital.

But the complications in this area of human conduct were nothing to the tangle in the other one, of homosexual behaviour between men, which was at that time, of course, illegal. Nobody had any idea how much of it there was, because it was, for obvious reasons, normally conducted in private. But there was an impression that it was increasing; and there was a feeling that if it was it ought to be curbed. The reasons here were quite different from those in the case of prostitution. There, the objection was to the public and flagrant nature of the soliciting: here, the objection was to what was widely called 'unnatural vice', which was thought to be degrading to the individual and to society. Here again there was a danger that the law might fall into disrespect because of the differing attitudes of different police forces up and down the country. In some places they took no steps unless something blatant was brought to their notice: in others they campaigned against homosexuals and even, it was darkly hinted, employed *agents provocateurs*. There was also ample opportunity for blackmail, compounded by the danger that if a man who was being blackmailed revealed the fact to the police he might be charged and sentenced for homosexual offences.

The Home Secretary's problems had lately been brought to a head by two cases which had attracted considerable public notice. So there was a very odd atmosphere. The vast majority of the population were probably unaware that there was such a thing as a homosexual offence; of the aware minority a majority regarded the whole business as distasteful and shocking, while a few were tolerant and sympathetic. In any case, the law itself might be said to be in rather a mess. There had never been legislation in Britain about homosexual behaviour between women, which perhaps explained why so many people thought that the 'homo-' part of 'homosexual' meant 'man'. Some sexual acts were offences against the law, whether homosexually or heterosexually conducted. The vulnerability of men had been widened by an extraordinary legislative accident when in 1885 Labouchere had introduced in the House of Commons on a Bill designed for the protection of women and girls an amendment which made any act of gross indecency between men an offence; the clause was passed by the House without any discussion of its substance and the amendment became and had since remained law.

In short, the Home Secretary thought that both these areas ought to be thoroughly examined. It was not his official business to set himself up as a censor of morals. But it was his business to be concerned with the administration of the law and with the civil liberties of citizens. What he had in mind was to set up a committee, widely representative of the relevant interests, to do a comprehensive review of these tricky areas and make what recommendations it thought fit. And would I, please, be chairman of it?

I have been asked a good many times why this particular lot fell on me. I have replied, with perfect truthfulness, that I don't know, adding, with equal truthfulness, that it cannot have been because I was an expert in either of these two subjects. I suppose it is not unreasonable to guess that if a government wants somebody to examine as objectively and dispassionately as possible some area which is likely to be controversial it is not a bad thing to look to the universities to provide him. If there is need of special technical knowledge it is probably better that that should be provided by individual experts, either as committee members or as witnesses, than by the chairman himself. And a certain amount of previous experience of chairing committees may be an advantage. Anyhow, there it was, and I left the Home Office when I called there the following week with a firm invitation from the Secretary of State in my pocket.

It must be remembered that all the events of this chapter took place more than twenty years ago. In those days the topics with which we were to be concerned were not mentioned in polite society. Most ordinary people had never heard of homosexuality; and of those who had the great majority regarded it with something nearer to disgust than to understanding. More of them knew about prostitution; but that knowledge was more likely to be disclaimed than paraded. The way in which these subjects are treated nowadays, in plays, films, television programmes, the Press, and general conversation would have been unthinkable then. I am not arguing the respective merits or demerits of these two states of affairs: I am simply pointing out that an effort of memory or imagination is necessary to realise the difference between then and now.

So before I could accept this invitation there were people to be consulted. The announcement of the setting-up of the Committee, and of my chairmanship of it, would probably create some stir, and we must assess in advance, as best we could, the probable consequences. My wife, of course, knew of the midnight conversation on the sleeper train. But an official invitation to take on the job was rather different. There were the four children to consider, one at university, the other three at school. What might they have to put up with in comment from their contemporaries if their father got involved in 'this sort of thing'? What about the University of Reading? Apart from the amount of my time it would inevitably consume, would it rub off harmfully that the Vice-Chancellor was busying himself with such matters? Indeed, could there be snide sniggerings about the universities in general? My Chancellor at Reading was Lord Templewood, who as Sir Samuel Hoare had been one of the more enlightened and humane Home Secretaries of this century; he had no doubt where my duty lay. After a fair amount of heart-searching the unanimous conclusion was that the invitation should be accepted.

The next stage was the actual composition of the Committee. There were obviously a great many points of view which ought to be represented, religious, medical, legal, political, sociological, and it was very important that the Committee should not be all-male. If each of these interests were represented by one separate person the Committee would be much too big. So individuals were sought who possessed double, or even triple, qualifications – a Conservative Roman Catholic peer, a woman doctor, a Labour member of the House of Commons who was also a barrister, and so on. The Home Office had already done some ingenious thinking along these lines, and it was not long before we were complete and in existence.

We were a Departmental Committee, not, as is often errone-ously supposed, a Royal Commission. The reasons given for this particular status were two: first, the fact that the subject-matter of our enquiry fell within the governmental responsibility of one Department, the Home Office, and we therefore did not need the supra-departmental authority of a Royal Commission; secondly, the very sensible fear that if we were bound by a Royal Commission's traditional practice of publishing evidence submitted to it we might well deprive ourselves of evidence which would be very important to us but intolerably embarrassing, if it were made public, to those who had given it. There may have been a third reason, that the government of the day had no wish to dignify with Royal Com-mission procedure the topics with which we were to deal. There was the incidental advantage that the initials of a Committee on

Homosexual Offences and Prostitution provided us with a conveniently brief and uninformative acronym: references to CHOP could bring no blush to any secretarial cheek.

This is perhaps an appropriate place to pay my own personal tribute to those who were my colleagues for nearly three years. Their devotion was complete, their patience unwearying, and their industry unflagging. Of course not everybody agreed with everybody about everything. But we did somehow develop a remarkable corporate spirit, and throughout those years, in areas often distasteful and sometimes embarrassing, with precious little chance of light-hearted relief, nobody, so far as I can remember, lost heart or lost his temper. The same goes for the small and dedicated secretariat and for the shorthand-writers who in the strictest confidence transcribed hundreds of thousands of words of oral evidence; they deserved more than the little party we gave them on the day of the publication of the report.

So we came to our first meeting – 'Vice, sir? Room 101,' said the door-keeper at the Home Office entrance – and the beginning of a remarkable collective experience for all of us. We were, with very few exceptions, strangers to each other. There had been a good deal of publicity about our appointment, and the normal amount of criticism. Now we had to get down to it. I ventured to make three preliminary observations, I hope not too pompously.

'(i) I have not the faintest idea at this moment what we shall ultimately recommend. But whatever it turns out to be my guess is that it will be unwelcome to approximately fifty per cent of Her Majesty's subjects. In short, we can't win. So it is no good looking over our shoulders all the time at what the Press will say about us at the end of the day. It is our business to listen to expert evidence, to exercise our judgments and follow our consciences, wherever they may lead.

(ii) I hope that when we come to write our report we may be able to produce a document which will not only be of some use to the Home Secretary and the Secretary of State for Scotland but will also be capable of being read and understood by any ordinarily intelligent citizen.

(iii) I hope that we may be able to establish among ourselves one or two general principles to guide us through these complicated affairs, so that our ultimate recommendations, whatever they are, hang together logically and are not just an accidental collection of isolated and unconnected items.'

It was also important to establish what we were not there to do. Our terms of reference required us 'to consider (a) the law and practice relating to homosexual offences and the treatment of persons convicted of such offences by the courts; and (b) the law and practice relating to offences against the criminal law in connection with prostitution and solicitation for immoral purposes; and to report what changes, if any, are in our opinion desirable.' In both parts of the job we were to consider 'the law and practice'. So from the start it was clear, or ought to have been, that we were concerned with the law. We were not concerned with homosexuality as a state or condition, except in so far as that was relevant to the treatment of those who had already been convicted by the courts. We were not concerned with prostitution as a social phenomenon, except in so far as there were offences against the criminal law in connection with it and with solicitation for immoral purposes. We were not there to write a sociological treatise or a handbook of moral theology or a textbook for medical students.

But it was not as simple as that, as we very soon found. There are obviously areas in which morality and the law overlap. Indeed, there were those who maintained, in their memoranda to us, that the two were, or ought to be, identical; the law's function, we were told, was to assert, defend, enforce morality – that is what the law is for. Oppositely, it was argued that in matters of personal morality the law should have no place at all unless and until immoral behaviour endangered society at large. It seemed to me that this was a fundamental question on which we must clear our minds as soon as we could. We were not, with two or three notable exceptions, lawyers, still less jurists; but if we were to produce any coherent pattern of recommendations we could not shut our eyes to these differences of doctrine, each supported by powerful and authoritative names.

So I thought the best thing to do was to go straight to the top. The Lord Chief Justice, Lord Goddard, had had a grandson at Shrewsbury, and I had from time to time seen and talked with him there. I therefore felt that I could appeal to him for help, in general on the Committee's concerns and in particular about this one.

Would he be willing to come and talk to us, as informally as he might wish, on this problem of the relation between morality and the law? Nothing could have been more generous than his response to this potentially embarrassing invitation. Goddard had the reputation of being harsh, uncompromising, even brutal. With us he was gentle, generous and in every way helpful. He readily agreed when I asked him if he would be our first oral witness, with this problem as the major topic for discussion.

It was quite an entertaining moment for an utter layman when I found the Lord Chief Justice of England sitting on the other side of the table, with me in charge and him in the witness-box. After the proper courtesies I laid our problem simply before him. We had had put to us these diametrically opposed opinions about the relationship between morality and the law. Could he help us by giving us his views on the connection between them? What was it that the criminal law stood for? In short – he must forgive me if this was an inept form of words – what sort of actions ought to be crimes? Long silence. He stroked his chin and watched the pigeons fluttering down into the Home Office courtyard. Then, slowly and apologetically, 'That is a question which in that form I cannot answer.' He meant, I think, that his business was not to make the laws but to interpret and apply them. Feeling slightly rebuffed, and with all my colleagues sitting round me in a rather embarrassed silence, I stammered, 'Yes – yes – I quite understand – foolish of me – forgive me. I wonder, though, if you could possibly put the question into a form in which you could answer it – and then answer it?' And off we went.

Rayner Goddard is not to be held responsible for any of the views which the Committee ultimately expressed. But he did get us off to a splendid start in the important exercise of clearing our minds, taking our bearings, setting our course, getting ourselves into context, whatever you like to call it; and I am abidingly grateful to him. I ought to be equally grateful to an anonymous small boy at Uppingham. He was hauled in to me one day by an infuriated form master, having been caught red-handed in the normal schoolboy crime of copying the answers off the book of the boy next to him. He did not deny the facts. Condign punishment was demanded. Before I inflicted it I asked, as was normal, if he had anything to say. He replied, as was not normal, 'Yes, sir, I have.' Taken slightly aback, I asked him what. 'Sir, there is no school rule against it, sir.' Years later, in Room 101 in the Home Office, in the presence of the Lord Chief Justice, there came back to me that very practical expression of one young person's ingenious if not wholly ingenuous identification of morality with the law.

Two of our next oral witnesses were also the outcome of Goddard's helpfulness. I had asked him if he could with propriety add two further favours to his personal visit to us. Would he feel able to ask the Judges of Assize whether from their own experience and knowledge they thought there ought to be any change in the law in the areas with which we were concerned? And, secondly, if their views differed, would he be prepared to nominate to appear before us one who held that the law ought to be enforced as it stood and one who held that it ought to be changed? He readily agreed to both requests. And we therefore had the privilege, and the intellectual pleasure, of conversation with two of Her Majesty's Judges, each propounding a view totally different from that of the other, and each claiming to express the opinion of a majority of his colleagues. It was hardly surprising that if the experts disagreed to this extent we poor innocents hardly knew whether we were coming or going.

And so it went on, for two crowded years. We read mountains of memoranda submitted as written evidence; and we interviewed dozens of oral witnesses. We did honestly try to include all those who thought they had a message for us, whether they were aiming to be 'objective' or were explicitly 'subjective'. We visited Edinburgh and learnt some surprising facts about that staid and sober city. We talked with police chiefs from the Provinces. We read transcripts of the evidence given in scores of cases where prosecutions had been brought – and pretty sickening reading it was. We interviewed individuals whose fictitious names I had to remember when I addressed them across the table. From time to time facetious gossip-column writers asked if we were undertaking first-hand experience in the relevant fields. For my part I thought it prudent to avoid public lavatories in the West End.

There were precious few occasions of light relief. One occurred when a highly respectable society of lawyers arranged for a party of girls from the streets to come and expound their point of view. My colleagues were looking forward with naughty expectation to my conduct of this particular interview, and were more than usually fertile in their suggestions about questions which might be asked. A few hours before it was due the visit was called off by the girls themselves. They had not realised that they would have to come to the Home Office, and they were not going to be seen dead entering or leaving that place. Besides, they thought it would be bad for trade, whereas I had supposed that these particular ones would acquire a cachet (if the word may be allowed) that others would lack. So that piece of first-hand experience was denied us.

Eventually we reached the point of embarking on a first draft of a report. The Home Office and the Scottish Office provided us with the necessary factual information about their respective laws and procedures: exposition, assessment and possible recommendations were clearly the responsibility of the Committee. Individual members submitted drafts of sections which might fall within their own professional specialisms; but the bulk of composition naturally fell to the Chairman and the Secretary. In accordance with my pronouncements at the outset I was anxious that the report should be readable and that it should be logical and internally consistent. I was also anxious that if we could we should avoid submitting majority and minority reports, because I did not think that to do that would be very helpful to our Secretaries of State. This did not, of course, mean that differences of opinion inside the Committee should be ignored, blurred or suppressed. By concentrating into a few paragraphs items on which we were not unanimous (and there were not many) we enabled all the members to sign the report as a whole, entering reservations on only the paragraphs which they could not accept. Mr Adair, for example, dissented from the paragraphs which contained our major recommendation about homosexual offences but was very willing to sign all the rest: and our medical members had professional views which they wished to put on record as refinements of the general position; and so on.

I took responsibility for drafting the chapter which set out our general approach and the underlying philosophy we had reached. Every sentence in the final document has a history, of discussion, rewording, expansion, deletion, fresh approach, and eventual acceptance. Our invaluable Secretary came to Reading many times between meetings, and once to where we were holidaying in South Wales. One of the difficulties was that if the whole thing was to hang together 'farming-out' around the members was not easy; and if one bit was re-drafted after discussion the rest had to be brought into line. All this is, I know, normal for committees and their chairmen; but perhaps this was a case, from the controversial nature of our topics and the considerable number of interests involved, where the demands were rather more rigorous than usual.

The day came for our last meeting (the sixty-second) when we hoped to sign the final version of the report. There were, even at the last minute, verbal tidyings-up. But it was duly signed, with the reservations I have mentioned, and we all made our way from the Home Office to the United University Club in Suffolk Street for a drink or two and a speech or two. We had lived through a good deal together and friendships had been made which still persist. The typescript now went to our Secretaries of State for their advance information and to Her Majesty's Stationery Office to be formally prepared for printing.

Our major recommendations can be summarised very briefly. First, we proposed a substantial increase in the maximum penalty for persistent soliciting. The existing flat rate of forty shillings seemed to us to be ludicrous, for reasons I have mentioned earlier; it had been fixed a hundred years earlier when forty shillings was a not inconsiderable sum, and quite clearly it was not a deterrent. So we recommended progressively higher fines for repeated offences, with an ultimate maximum of three months' imprisonment. The purpose of this last rather stern proposal was twofold. Its first object was straightforward deterrence. But there was another one as well. As the law then stood, a probation order could be made only if the offender expressed willingness to comply with its imposition and conditions. With the alternative to probation a nugatory fine most prostitutes expressed their preference in pretty pungent terms. Our hope was that with the alternative a possible spell in prison more of them might be willing at any rate to see and listen to a probation officer. We may have been misguided or over-optimistic: but it is not the case that we were being viciously vindictive or blindly draconian.

On the second half of our remit our proposals were a good deal more radical. Here we proposed, quite simply, that homosexual behaviour between consenting adults in private be no longer a criminal offence. We did not explicitly define 'consent' and 'in private', leaving these words to be interpreted as they would be in the case of heterosexual acts: we suggested, after a great deal of argument, that the age of adulthood for these purposes should be twenty-one; and we tried to relieve from the threat of prosecution the victim of blackmail who revealed homosexual behaviour. We also, as is sometimes forgotten, recommended an increase in the penalties for gross indecency between a man over twenty-one and a partner below that age.

When they had read the typescript, ministers and senior Home Office officials warned me that there might well be considerable reactions from various quarters and advised me to be ready for public criticism and perhaps prolonged argument. My wife and I had arranged to take our two younger children to Guernsey for a late summer holiday, and it was touch and go whether HMSO would have the printed report ready in time for me to get it off my plate before we went.

On the evening of Monday, September 2nd, 1957, I walked across from the Home Office to the House of Commons with an armful of copies, the Home Office public relations folk in attendance, to meet the Lobby correspondents. It had been expected that the meeting would take half an hour or so. It took two hours. I had spent the week-end going through the report and marking the passages which I thought would be of most interest; so I was able to take them through it without undue waste of their time and without their missing anything of importance. I need not say that the Lobby behaved with its usual discretion, penetration and responsibility.

It is difficult for me, and it must be nearly impossible for anybody else, to realise the to-do that followed. It entirely filled the front pages of Wednesday's evening papers, with VICE in inch-high capitals as the main headline. And Thursday's dailies, in their different styles, gave it more column-inches than any of us had dreamt of. Naturally some of them concentrated on what they could pick out as 'sensational'; but the striking thing was the balanced and responsible nature of the presentation of the actual contents of the report. It was rather different with the editorial comment, which was extensive. Here there came to light the extreme, indeed sometimes violent, differences of opinion which our recommendations provoked. The *Daily Express* called it 'cumbersome nonsense'; the *Daily Telegraph* said that, 'The Committee's findings, though necessarily controversial, are clear, conscientious and courageous'; the

Evening Standard said that our recommendations on homosexuality were 'bad, retrograde and utterly to be condemned'; the *Daily Mail* called them 'proposals to legalise degradation in our midst'; and so on. Broadly, though not unanimously, the recommendations about 'cleaning up the streets' were approved; but the recommendations about homosexual offences were harder to swallow. Most of the Sunday papers, having had a little longer to think and to gauge immediate reactions, went rather more deeply into the fundamental question of the law's relation to morality, counselling sober and serious reflection before any positive action was taken. John Gordon, not surprisingly, called the report 'The Pansies' Charter'. I enjoyed the high privilege of being officially cursed, out of the blue, by Jehovah through the typewriter of His Prophet George. My only regret was that I was sent not the original but a carbon copy: do originals of such documents go up the chimney in flames, like petitions to Santa Claus – or what?

For me and the family there was no more holiday. Our quiet little Guernsey hotel was invaded by BBC interviewers, journalists flown in to take photographs and a sudden blaze of notoriety. I had to come back and talk to newspapers, parliamentarians and television interrogators.

It went on for weeks. The *Daily Mirror* conducted a poll of its readers. Archbishops supported us, correspondence columns thrived, cartoonists had their fun, street-walkers talked to the Press, obscenities were chalked on the pavement outside our house in Reading. Gradually the almost hysterical uproar died down, and people began to ask what, if anything, the Government was going to do about it.

They were not, understandably enough, in a tearing hurry to do anything. The John Gordon view might well represent the attitude of quite a substantial section of grass-roots opinion in the constituencies; and why should any government go out of its way to lose votes by quixotically championing an unpopular minority? (Friends of mine in the Labour Party did not deny that they would have taken the same line if they had been in office.) The whole business became, in its small way, a political hot potato; it was not surprising that they should take a little time to assess its precise temperature.

Meanwhile the public opinion debate, as distinct from the parliamentary or political one, went on. Not everybody understood that the two halves of our recommendations were governed by the same logic. We had argued, to put it very briefly, that since one of the law's concerns was the preservation of public order and decency, steps should be taken to remove the affront to public order and decency which was presented by the obtrusive presence of large numbers of prostitutes openly soliciting in the streets. At the same time we argued that private morality or immorality was a private affair, and therefore that 'there must remain a realm of private morality and immorality which is, in brief and crude terms, not the law's business'. It followed, or so it seemed to us, that while steps should be taken to clear the streets of soliciting prostitutes, the behaviour of consenting adult males in private was their affair and not the law's. The attacks on this simple proposition were many, various and not always mutually consistent. When we urged that soliciting prostitutes should be kept off the streets we were told that we were 'simply brushing it under the carpet', 'it' being 'sexual vice'. The reply was, in accordance with our basic proposition, that what a man and a woman chose to do in private was no concern of ours or anybody else's, but that public solicitation on the then prevalent scale was; that we were not so simple-minded as to suppose that prostitution could be abolished by law; and that there were some things which were better swept under the carpet than lying about on top of it.

We were accused by some highly respectable women's organisations of discriminating against the prostitute and doing nothing about her wicked client. Indeed, one very distinguished ecclesiastic charged me with this in conversation. 'Surely,' he said, 'you would agree that the man who goes with a prostitute is just as guilty as she is.' To which I replied, 'My dear Archbishop, he may be just as guilty as she is of what you and I might call the sin of fornication: he is not as guilty as she is of the offence of cluttering up the streets of London.' The ambiguities which spring from words like 'guilty' were not easily resolved. Nor were our withers wrung by prophecies that to get the girls off the streets would inevitably lead to increases in call-girl networks, strip-clubs and other clandestine channels of assignation. We were not concerned with prostitution as such or with immorality as such: we stuck to our last of public order and decency.

There was a debate in the House of Lords three months after the publication of the report, which by then had sold fifteen thousand copies. All the obvious points were made, with demands for ruthless suppression of 'evil men', and for prosecuting the customers of prostitutes. At the same time the Archbishop of Canterbury bravely asserted that 'The right to decide one's own moral code – even to man's own hurt – is a fundamental right given by God.' The debate ranged widely and ended inconclusively. Broadly, the Government's intention was that more time should be allowed for consideration and discussion of the recommendations on homosexual behaviour but that they would see what could be done about clearing the streets. Some sections of the Press expressed sharp impatience: others rejoiced that our subversive proposals were so admirably resisted. At least the Lords' debate served the purpose of ventilating the problems and helping Press and public to appreciate them. It was now respectable to talk about these things, and it became increasingly possible to discuss them without hysteria.

Eventually, in November 1958, rather more than a year after we had reported, Rab Butler, as Home Secretary, opened a Commons debate. He felt that the Government would not be justified in introducing legislation in the homosexual field, since an alteration in the existing law would be regarded by many as implying approval or tolerance of what they regarded as a great social evil. But he hinted that legislation was being prepared to 'clean up the streets'; and in the following summer the Street Offences Act became law.

I had not thought it my business to campaign about legislation on either of the two parts of the report. I have spent a good deal of time, from the day of publication right down to the present, in trying to expound and explain it, to audiences of magistrates, doctors, undergraduates and learned societies; and I have been led further and further into discussions, in less professional circles, of the respective spheres of morality and the law, or, more snappily, Crime and Sin. But I have declined all invitations to join pressure-groups of any kind. My job, the Committee's job, was to 'consider' these problems and to report what changes in the law, if any, we might think desirable. It was for other people, in their turn, to take over from there and to consider what we proposed: it was not, in my judgment, my business to wave banners. I may have been wrong. Certainly not all chairmen of comparable committees have taken this line; some of them have preferred advocacy to exposition. But I think a degree of detachment, once the committee is discharged, is right. At that point its job is done and it properly says to the Government and Parliament, 'Over to you'.

On the homosexual front Parliament showed no great urgency. In the summer of 1960 there was a free vote on an Opposition motion to change the law in accordance with our recommendations. It was resoundingly defeated. Other debates followed, at lengthening intervals but with decreasing majorities against changing the law. In 1965 a renewed initiative came from what some might have regarded as the unlikeliest possible quarter. The Earl of Arran, with great personal courage and inspired by a flaming zeal to remove what he regarded as a shameful injustice to a persecuted minority, persuaded the House of Lords to initiate legislation for this purpose. Eighteen months later, on the initiative of Mr Leo Abse, the Commons followed suit. And in the summer of 1967 the Sexual Offences Act came into effect, giving legal form to the recommendations we had made almost exactly ten years earlier.

I have often been asked if I was not disappointed that these 'reforms' took so long. I have always answered, I think honestly, that I was not – for two reasons. First, the sapient Permanent Secretary at the Home Office said to me, when he had read the draft of our report, 'Don't expect legislation quickly. In a thing like this, where deep emotions are likely to be aroused, I would guess fourteen years as the average time-lag between recommendations and legislation.' Secondly, on a quite different wavelength, I had been in the United States when the Prohibition laws were in force. I saw then what happens when legislation is out of sympathy with public opinion, and the general disrepute into which the law falls if it is almost universally disregarded. There can be plenty of argument about whether the law should lead or follow public opinion. It may well be that in matters of international relationships or national economic policy the government of the day should give a lead and bring the public along behind it. But it may also well be that in sensitive matters of private behaviour any government should wait until public opinion is ready for any steps any government might take. Far better to wait a year or two and act with public opinion behind you than to leap in and find yourself out of tune with it. Certainly public opinion, as reflected in Parliament, changed very considerably over those ten years. When I originally presented the report to ministers, I was told, 'Extremely interesting: but, you

Olu's christening at Reading, 1958

Lord Templewood, as Chancellor of Reading University, presents to The Queen pages of accounts of the Royal Household from the 18th century, 1957

'The House of Lords discusses the Wolfenden Report'.
A Punch cartoon of 11 December 1957

'Thank you, Professor. Would you take a seat outside while we discuss your application?' David Langdon's original was presented to me after it had appeared in *Punch* on 19 February 1964

know, you are way out in front of public opinion.' By the end of ten years it had caught up.

Are these all 'old, unhappy, far-off things, and battles long ago'? Unhappy – no. I do not regret what we said and what happened thereafter. I personally got landed with a label which has probably been more embarrassing to my children than to me. At one time there was a rumour that our rather distinctive surname had passed into some Middle European languages as meaning a practising adult male homosexual. My legal friends, half-seriously, told me to watch out for anything similar in English and offered their services free in a libel action which would, they promised, set me up for life. But unfortunately English newspapers and magazines are too efficiently advised by their legal experts. One New York publisher rang me up, five years after the report was published, to say that he had bought the text from Her Majesty's Stationery Office and would I go over to do some launching speeches? My saying 'No' did not discourage him from ringing again six months later to say that he had now done a deal with a paperback publisher, so that this epoch-making sociological document could be on sale in every drugstore throughout the United States; would I go over to do some launching speeches? I again said 'No', but added that I would like to have, if he could spare them, a copy of each of these publications. When they arrived I found that the title was not HMSO's formal 'Report of the Committee on Homosexual Offences and Prostitution' but 'The Wolfenden Report'. Perhaps I should have sued him. The contract, of course, was made not with me but with HMSO, who in such cases are 'the author'; no penny came to me, but I hope HMSO collected a decent number of dollars for what, by their standards, had turned out to be a best-seller.

I confess that one incident did nettle me. Among my quite considerable mail came a letter from a total stranger, who said that he did not suppose that what I actually wrote in reports, or what happened as a result, was of any real interest to me, so long as I made a fat living out of the huge sums which I was obviously receiving from public funds. Actually, of course, we (quite rightly) received nothing but our bare expenses, and there were no fees or royalties for any of us from the publication of the report. I suppose it cost me a couple of hundred pounds in journeys and hospitality which I did not feel justified in charging to the tax-payer.

Far-off – yes. It all seems a long time ago. I can entirely understand the frame of mind of those young men and women who
within recent years have come to interview me for one or other of
the media. 'But it's all so old-fashioned, isn't it? I've just read the
report again, and some of it seems positively Victorian. What on
earth was all the fuss about?' Fine, if that is how it strikes them. It
may well be that it is time to review the whole field again, that
further changes are due, in one place or another; after nearly twenty
years that would not be unreasonable. What I find amusing is that
we, who were thought by many to be so outrageous in 1957, should
now be regarded as Victorian fuddy-duddies. It is entertaining to
have lived long enough to have made oneself obsolete.

9

The University Grants Committee

[1963]

I stayed at Reading longer than I had intended – indeed, longer than in any other job, before or since. It was not easy to see where there was to go from there. There had been vague talk of the headship of an Oxford college, but nothing materialised; I did not particularly want to go to another university, in Britain or the Commonwealth, because I did not see myself transplanting to another place our affection for Reading; offers from outside the university world had always seemed either inappropriate or untimely. And I suppose a certain degree of notoriety still hung over from 'the Report'.

In the end, the suggestion that I might become Chairman of the University Grants Committee answered all the problems. It was a highly responsible job, especially just at that time; I knew personally all the vice-chancellors with whom I should have dealings; I had had a certain amount to do with the Civil Service; and there was every prospect of being kept busy, in a pretty hot seat, for the rest of my working life.

The University Grants Committee is a remarkable example of the way the British have of evolving institutions and procedures which on the face of it cannot possibly work but which in practice are far more effective than the tidier and more logical constructions of others. It must be comparatively easy to run a system where the Government directly controls the universities and the academic staffs are in effect civil servants. But in Britain that is not the pattern. There are powerful and deep-seated (if not very precisely defined) concepts like 'academic freedom' and 'university autonomy' to be reckoned with. On the other hand there is 'the public interest', as represented by public opinion, Parliament and the government of the day; and when those influences are expressed in terms of very substantial financial provision for the universities by the tax-payer they have to be reckoned with too. So there are continuous and healthy tensions; and at the centre of them is the UGC and, in particular, its chairman.

Some people seem to think (or used to) that the UGC is a fairy godmother generously handing out to the universities all the money they think they want. It is not always realised that the first thing the UGC has to do is to get the money from the Government; and in all the competition there is for public money that is a considerable task. Very briefly, the procedure is this. Universities are asked to submit to the UGC, once every five years, a detailed account of their expected income and their hoped-for expenditure for each year of the forthcoming quinquennium, distinguishing between capital spending and annual recurrent costs. Their income, for these purposes, includes income from endowments, investments, rents, students' fees, research contracts – everything except what they have in former years received from the UGC. Their expenditure includes the salaries of the academic and administrative staff, wages of laboratory technicians, books for the library, laboratory equipment, maintenance of buildings and grounds. The income is 'expected', because it is within narrow limits predictable: the expenditure is 'hoped-for' because it will not be realised without a massive contribution from UGC funds towards it. Students' fees, paid in part by local authorities and in part by parents, not by the UGC, cover less than one-tenth of what a student actually costs. (Halls of residence and other forms of university-managed student accommodation, once built, are required to be self-supporting and do not enter into the annual balance sheet.) Capital spending is, obviously, the cost of a new laboratory or library or residential hall.

Plainly, the gap between expected income and hoped-for expenditure is enormous, especially in a period of expansion. That is the gap which the UGC is concerned with and that is the amount of money which is the meat of each university's submission. What the UGC does not do is add up all the submissions from the universities and transmit them to the Government. It combs through the figures for each university, with one friendly eye and one critical one; its officials have long and detailed discussions with the vice-chancellors and finance officers of each; its own expert sub-committees are consulted; and after weeks or months of patient toil a final total sum for the universities as a whole is submitted to the Government. For this total the UGC, not the universities, takes the responsibility and conducts the necessary arguments with those who guard the public purse. Eventually an agreement is reached on the total; and it then becomes the UGC's task to carve up the cake among the individual universities. Of course, nobody is ever satisfied. The Government, or the Treasury, regard the demands as excessive: the universities, collectively and individually, regard the sums they receive as inadequate. And the UGC takes the knock from both sides. One of the senior officials of the UGC coined the splendidly descriptive phrase that we operated on the Principle of Equal and Opposite Unpopularity. If we were popular with the Government we should be suspected of being in their pocket; if we were popular with the universities we should be suspected of being in theirs; if we were equally unpopular with both we were probably just about right. A cruder way of putting it was that ours was the backside for everybody to kick.

Two principles of the allocation to the individual universities were cardinal. The first was that the annual recurrent income (though not the capital expenditure) was on a quinquennial basis. That is to say that once every five years each university was told what its grant from public funds would be for each of the next five years, so that it could plan ahead with reasonable security. There are obvious weaknesses in this arrangement. Since the allocation is made only once in five years, a university's view of its future is shortened every year until the next quinquennium comes along; there is (or was in my time) insufficient recognition of the effect on recurrent costs of completed capital programmes and the new buildings they brought into use; and in a period of steep inflation what looked like an adequate grant when it was made turns out to be quite inadequate four or five years later. Nevertheless, with all these shortcomings the system gives the universities some safeguards against repeated 'stop-and-go'. I have no doubt that since my time it has been refined and improved.

The second cardinal principle was that the recurrent allocation was made to each university as a block grant. The university's original quinquennial submission to the UGC was itemised and detailed, and was scrutinised item by item and detail by detail. But at the end of the day the university received an unitemised block grant, for the deployment of which it alone was responsible, through its own annual autonomous internal budgetary procedures. The universities, in short, were trusted to spend their money prudently – after all, it paid them to do so. They were not subjected to item-by-item matching of each detail against the estimate. This trust in the responsibility of the universities as corporate spenders is a remarkable example of the liberal regard which governments of all parties have constantly shown for academic autonomy.

Capital expenditure was dealt with rather differently. The funds for it were allocated by Parliament on an annual, not on a quinquennial basis. (Of course, the quinquennial allocations for recurrent grant were constitutionally dependent on an annual provision by Parliament; but we all confidently assumed that once the quinquennial totals had been approved Parliament would do its stuff year by year.) So we had a separate annual argument about capital expenditure, with lists of projected buildings compared, costed and scrutinised by the UGC's expert and hideously over-worked staff of architects. It was not the UGC's business to commission, still less to design, university buildings: that was for the universities themselves to do. But as costs rose, and in the population explosion which burst on us after Robbins, somebody obviously had to take a central look both at the comparative claims of separate universities and at the absolute total we were requesting from the tax-payer. It was necessary to introduce 'norms', namely, the appropriate standards of size, material, and finish for a particular kind of building, laboratory, library, hall of residence, or whatever. These were not popular with the universities. But we had to be able to satisfy ourselves, the Government and Parliament that there was no extravagance involved. It happened that as I moved from Reading to the UGC's offices in Belgrave Square I was in the middle of a passionate controversy with the UGC on an issue very similar to this one, so that, as in a game of progressive ping-pong, I was (almost) running round the net to return my own shot.

There was one administrative complication about the capital programme which on one occasion had an unexpected consequence. When any building project was sanctioned the whole ultimate cost of that building was reckoned in to the UGC budget for the year in which it started. So from the point of view of annual accounting we were talking about 'starts', not 'spends'. One day this came in useful. My current Secretary of State asked me to go and see him urgently one afternoon. Gravely he explained that he had been required to make a substantial cut in his budget for the coming financial year, and, of course, the universities would have to face their fair proportion of it. That I could not deny. His conclusion was that we should have to dock the universities' recurrent grant for next year. I ventured to point out that to do that would mean sacking university staff, at some level or other, and abandoning the quinquennial principle to which everybody, including himself, constantly said they attached so much importance. With a shade of impatience he asked me what possible alternative there was. I said there was no problem. As he knew, the capital programme was on an annual basis of 'starts'. If it should happen that the beginning of a new Physics Department somewhere slipped by a couple of days from one financial year into the next, he would have 'saved' a million pounds straight off. Anyhow, there was no need to contrive such a postponement; it always did happen anyway that starts slipped, by reason of delays entirely outside our control. So he was home and dry, without any sacrifice of principle, saved by book-keeping.

It is not to be supposed that the universities had it all their own way or that they could do just what they liked with the tax-payer's money which came to them from the fairy godmother's cornucopia. The tradition I inherited was that the UGC was a 'buffer' in this context. Obviously it was not a buffer in the sense of being the point at the end of the platform where the locomotive comes to rest. So presumably it was a buffer-state, a neutral area subjected to pressures from two opposite sides and absorbing both. Certainly it was and always had been part of the UGC's function to be interposed between the Government, any government, and the universities, individually and collectively. It owed its origin and its continued life to the accepted principle that public money should flow into the universities but no political pressure on them or governmental intervention in them should be tolerated. Something not so wholly passive as 'buffer' might have been a more appropriate description: even shock-absorber, or transformer, or go-between, or honest broker. I did once hear the UGC described as a septic tank, through which filthy Treasury money passed and emerged as a crystal-clear liquid which even a professor might drink without risk. But any job-description on that sort of level, especially when the sums of money involved were comparatively small, became not only inadequate but positively misleading when we were talking in terms of nearly two hundred million pounds a year. The point was dramatically made during my first month.

I took up office, in a beautiful room in one of the stateliest houses in Belgrave Square, on October 1st, 1963. On October 23rd the Robbins Report was published, with weighty reasons for a vast expansion of the universities. On October 24th it was accepted in principle by the Government. On October 25th I attended a meeting of the Committee of Vice-Chancellors and Principals (whose last meeting I had attended as a member) to enlist their support for the Robbins proposals. The expansion envisaged was gigantic. Apart altogether from any doctrines anybody might hold about making available to a wider clientele what had hitherto been regarded as the privilege of an élite, the simple facts of demography were compelling. It should surprise nobody that within a couple of years after the end of a long war there is a spectacular jump in the birth-rate. For years this 'bulge', as it was ungracefully called, had been moving up the schools, and was now approaching university age. On current standards of university admission – and they were admittedly difficult to define with precision – vastly more young people than ever before were now about to reach those standards, simply because age-groups were so much bigger. Why should younger brothers and sisters, with the same academic qualifications as their elders, be deprived of a university education simply because through no fault of their own they belonged to bigger age-groups? That was one straightforwardly quantitative reason for providing more university places. The other, side by side with the 'bulge', was the 'trend'. There was becoming apparent throughout secondary education a trend for young people to stay at school longer and so to take in greatly increasing numbers the examinations which qualified them for university admission. The combination of Brother Bulge with Brother Trend was irresistible.

I asked the assembled vice-chancellors to consult inside their respective universities and to let me know, within the next five weeks, what each of them could do to meet this explosive situation.

Understandably enough, their immediate reactions differed *inter se*. If after years of carefully planned growth you have got your university to what you regard as just about the right size, with just about the right balance between various fields of study and with just about the right proportion of postgraduate to undergraduate populations, you are understandably reluctant to see all this knocked sideways by a sudden and relatively unplanned influx of undergraduates, especially when their qualifications are in fields in which you may not wish to expand. On the other hand, if you are a comparatively small university, whose proper growth has been in your view hampered by shortages of money and students, you may welcome an increase in numbers, especially if it enables you to start up departments of which you have hitherto been starved. We at the centre could only imagine, and tensely await, the debates that went on in faculty boards, senates and councils throughout the universities of the United Kingdom, well knowing that there are there, as there are anywhere else, conservatives and empire-builders, the ambitious and the timid. But I have no doubt that the prevailing sentiment was one of national duty, educational obligation, social justice, call it what you will. To their eternal credit the universities came up, in a very short time, with promises of expansion which in aggregate exceeded the need.

Of course, all this was not unforeseen. My predecessor at the UGC and his colleagues had already established seven brand-new universities. (They came to be known in some quarters as the 'Plate-glass' universities, as distinct from 'Oxbridge' and 'Redbrick'. Personally I preferred to think of them as the 'Shakespeares': if you recite some of their names – Canterbury, York, Lancaster, Warwick, Norwich – they might easily be a couple of lines from *King Henry IV, Part II*.) But it would be some time, in the ordinary course of events, before they grew to the size it was fashionable to call 'viable'. Opinions differed about the 'right' size for a university; but clearly it ought to be big enough to justify the inevitable overhead costs of administration and to provide at least the minimum spread of subjects essential to academic health. On the other hand, if their growth was suddenly and artificially accelerated by the injection of an unexpectedly large intake, could their academic digestions survive? They could not be expected to cope with the whole operation. The more firmly established institutions already had the necessary infrastructure, and on that too we must build. Mountains of money would be needed, and thousands of additional members of university staffs, in all grades.

The simple figures tell the expansion story dramatically enough. The total university population rose from 113,100 in 1962 to 184,700 in 1967 (and to 245,000 by 1973). This could not have been done simply by expanding the existing universities and hastening the growth of the Plate-glass Shakespeares. Both these operations went ahead as fast as money, buildings and additional staff could be provided; and we tried hard to preserve the individuality of each of the existing ones and to encourage each of the new ones to find and assert a distinctive ethos of its own.

There was a steady stream of municipal delegations petitioning that we would establish universities in their respective cities or boroughs. But we now had enough new foundations in England and Wales; the Shakespeares must be allowed to grow. Scotland was a different matter. It had been agreed that there should be one new university in Scotland; but its location had not been decided. We were subjected to an intelligent and high-pressure sales campaign by half a dozen places from Ayr to Inverness, including, from one enterprising Provost, a trip in a helicopter to enable us to see at a glance the advantages of the proposed site. Every possible argument, based on local patriotism, was deployed in each place. I myself was very tempted to try one of the New Towns, perhaps Cumbernauld, because I thought it would be a salutary experiment deliberately to put a new university in a New Town, as a change from cathedral cities. But I recognised that we were too late. If it had been possible to build in a new university right from the start of planning a New Town it might have worked: but they had now settled into their patterns, and a university would have been an artificial adjunct rather than an integral element in a new community. We finally plumped for Stirling. It had a history, it was near to Scotland's concentration of population, it had a good many big houses which could be used for student residence, and it had a beautiful site with lake and rolling parkland which reminded me of Reading. In retrospect, I think we were right.

Fortunately, there was at hand another source of new university places. The Colleges of Advanced Technology were institutions already carefully selected by the Ministry of Education, from the great army of technical colleges up and down the country, to serve as centres of technological education at the highest level. Eight of them in England and two in Scotland were 'accorded University status', with Royal Charters, and thenceforward granted their own degrees; the Welsh CAT in Cardiff became a College of the University of Wales; and the Chelsea College of Technology became a School of the University of London. Each of them, in consultation with the UGC, equipped itself with an Academic Advisory Committee, to plan its future development as a university and to plot a course between the Scylla of 'nothing but technology' and the Charybdis of 'being a university means doing everything'. My own rough-and-ready distinction was, 'By all means teach French and German to your scientists, as a tool of their trade. But we don't particularly want you to encourage people to come to you to read for an Honours Degree in Modern Languages. Nor would it make sense if the first appointment you advertised in your new status was for a Professor of Philosophy.' The new University of Stirling completed the picture. There was shortly to be a new University of Ulster too, but that was in a different category, since the UGC's writ did not run in Northern Ireland though its advice was frequently sought by successive ministers at Stormont and freely given.

All this did not happen without some upheaval in the existing universities. Economies of size may have their attractions. But very rapid expansion disrupts familiar patterns, knocks sideways deeply ingrained habits and sometimes overwhelms administration. Hundreds of additional lodgings had to be found, teaching accommodation improvised, new staff recruited. Senates grew to unwieldy size, laboratories had to get used to shift-working, relationships with Students' Unions became more complicated.

And there were some doctrinal criticisms as well. The universities had without doubt come to be regarded as institutions for an academic élite, and there was a perfectly genuine fear that if more and more people came to them standards were bound to fall, not only in the quality of the intake but also in the quality of the teaching. These fears, at any rate so far as the numerical intake was concerned, ought to have been answered by the Robbins evidence of sheer demography. And every effort was made to preserve the existing staff–student ratio – which was itself often criticised, from the opposite point of view, as being too liberal if not luxurious. It was, admittedly, difficult to find in a hurry the necessary number of additional junior staff; and the average age of professors dropped smartly as new Chairs were created in unprecedented numbers. But somehow it was managed, with more or less anguish and more or less smoothness.

The percentage of the relevant age-group moving from school to university was still appreciably lower than in many other countries. To set against this was, and is, the fact that our failure-rate is the lowest in the world; so that the percentage of entrants who become graduates is probably well up the league-table. That is indeed the main justification for a staff–student ratio which is the envy of other countries. I have often argued with friends in American universities that whatever their finances may permit, ours do not allow us to pay for the scarce and therefore expensive academic staffs needed to teach a student population of which only one-third will graduate. An apparently expensive staff-student ratio, combined with pretty rigorous standards of student admission, is a more economical way of conducting higher education. The riposte is that it can't do anybody any harm to go to university for one year or two, even if he or she does leave without a degree, can it? To which the answer is that that may be all right if you can afford it, but we can't.

I think it was probably at the point of the Robbins expansion that the traditional notion of the UGC as a buffer came to be recognised as inadequate, if not obsolete. In an expansion on this scale there had to be some sort of central strategic planning agency. Not all the universities were equally capable of rapid expansion in all directions at the same time. Not all of them could simultaneously be provided, at enormous public expense, with expensive buildings and equipment in the same fields. Not all of them ought to be encouraged to set themselves up in disciplines which were foreign to their individual traditions. But if there was to be such a strategic plan it must not transgress deep-seated doctrines about academic freedom and university autonomy. It must somehow be government by consent rather than by compulsion.

Fortunately, it was a built-in part of the UGC's history that a large majority of its members were practising academics. There were members, and very valuable they were, from other parts of the educational system and from business and industry. But essentially the UGC was a body of professors. It may seem odd, or 'typically British', that men who are, in fable at least, unworldly, unpractical and visionary, should be the chosen agents for the spending of millions of pounds of public money every year. In my experience the mythological adjectives were wildly inapposite; and anyway there was always in the background a small but highly skilled and deeply experienced staff of permanent officials. The real strength of the academic base of the UGC became very clear in this turmoil of expansion. Difficult decisions had to be made, some inevitably giving deep disappointment and some coming very near to the borders of university autonomy. But always these academic decisions were being made by academics, themselves as individual professors in individual universities as vulnerable to disappointment as anybody else. They knew where the shoe would pinch; when they went back home from a meeting in Belgrave Square they would find themselves as toads under the harrow they had fashioned there. And their colleagues throughout the universities, pained and sometimes angry as they might be, knew that the decisions had been made by academic colleagues, not by faceless men in Whitehall or by whizz-kids fiddling with computers. There were stresses and strains; and I expect there were mistakes; but the gradual transition from 'buffer' to 'strategy' came to be accepted, if not with enthusiasm at least with understanding and even some sympathy.

As part of this extension of our traditional function we ventured to issue to the universities, in 1967, what we called a 'Memorandum of General Guidance', to accompany the letter which announced to each university its annual recurrent grant for each year of the coming quinquennium. The memorandum was intended to convey to the universities the Committee's general policy about such matters as total numbers, the distribution between postgraduate and undergraduate courses, collaboration with industry, with other universities and with other sectors of the system of higher education; and we tried to indicate which disciplines seemed to us to demand encouragement and which were in danger of over-provision. We related each university's grant to its projected student numbers, in four categories, postgraduate Arts, postgraduate Science, undergraduate Arts and undergraduate Science, with a different price-tag on each. We were not telling each university how many students it was to have in each category or how much to spend on each student. We were telling them that this number of students at this cost was what we were providing the money for. The block grant remained a block grant, and it was for them to allocate it internally by their own procedures. Naturally, this was regarded by some as unwelcome interference with 'university autonomy' and we were accused of *dirigisme*. In one particular subject we went so far as to suggest that three universities might run down their Departments of Agriculture so that, as an independent government committee had recommended, agricultural students should be concentrated in fewer and bigger schools. We did not command these universities to stop teaching agriculture; we simply said that we were not going to provide the money for it. As I explained to each of the vice-chancellors concerned, if he could find the money from elsewhere, good luck to him. If this was *dirigisme* at least the directing hand wore a velvet glove.

And all this time there was the other partner in all this, the government of the day. When I first went there the UGC was directly linked to the Treasury, as it had been from its birth forty-five years before. But it had gradually become apparent that this was an anomalous arrangement. The Treasury is not by nature a spending department; and apart from logic there was the other practical issue that when the Treasury demanded cuts or savings from other departments its own spending on the universities could not go unchallenged. There was, further, a growing feeling that the universities ought not to continue to be kept in isolation from all the rest of the educational world. A pattern which might have been acceptable fifty years ago seemed outmoded in the conditions of the 1960s.

This long-standing connection with the Treasury had certainly been beneficial to the universities. Over the years there had grown up between Treasury ministers and officials, on the one side, and the UGC and the universities on the other, a mutual understanding and a community of outlook which made it easy to do business; both sides accepted the same principles and the only argument was about the application of them from one quinquennium to another. So it was with real regret on both sides that the arrangement had to be changed. The Robbins expansion gave the final push. Now that the amount of money involved was so big, what was suitable in the pre-war years was now hardly defensible in the public interest; and now that the universities were coming closer and closer to the educational system at large a special relationship for them alone seemed hardly defensible either.

After a brief sojourn under the wing of the Lord President of the Council we became the responsibility of the Department of Education and Science in 1964. There was considerable uneasiness in the universities about this translation. Accustomed to what they had come to regard as a fairly cosy relationship with Treasury civil servants who 'talked the same language', they did not enjoy the prospect of being in competition for funds with all the other members of the far-flung empire of the Department of Education and Science. Especially, they were afraid of a more heavy-handed or a more niggling approach by the Department's officials than they had been used to from the Treasury. I can only say that in my judgment, based on day-to-day experience of Ministers and officials, these fears were proved groundless. Indeed, I believe that successive Ministers, of whatever political party, argued the case for the universities with their Cabinet colleagues and with the Treasury more effectively than the UGC could have done alone. And all the senior officials of the Department leaned over backwards in their anxiety not to disrupt the admittedly unusual relationship which existed. I had, if memory serves, seven Ministers in my five years. They varied, inevitably, in their appreciation of the particular ethos of the universities and the UGC. But they became, if they were not already, almost more royalist than the King in their staunch defence of what was important in university autonomy and academic freedom. I am proud to have worked with them and their senior officials.

Another source of disquiet to the universities was a corollary of the new alignment, namely, the requirement that the finances of the UGC and of the universities should be opened to the scrutiny of the Comptroller and Auditor-General, with the consequent possibility of 'interference' from the Public Accounts Committee. Here again, in my experience, the fears were proved to be largely groundless, again because the officials concerned were as anxious as anybody not to disrupt a successfully going concern. To many of us it simply made sense that two hundred millions a year of public money should not only be, but be seen to be, spent economically and effectively. And, after all, the more efficiently the money was used, the greater the freedom of a university to carry out its own academic plans. In a variety of small ways the advice of the Comptroller and Auditor-General was practically useful; and, in my time at least, there was no sign of gratuitous interference or vexatious fussiness. My own infrequent appearances before the Public Accounts Committee were, if it is not impertinent to say so, enjoyable rather than scarifying.

One Minister, as St Paul said of stars, differs from another in glory. There was one who hit the table with his walking-stick when words failed him; there was one who always brought an armful of files when she came to lunch with me; there was one who signed off in the course of receiving a deputation to play over in his head a Mozart horn concerto; there was one with whom I sadly discussed a cut in university income for twenty minutes before I discovered that he was delicately trying to convey to me a cut half as big as I had expected and planned for; there was one who wanted to attend all meetings of the UGC so that he could see for himself what happened 'on the shop-floor'. One entertaining phenomenon was the recurring change in the furniture and pictures in the ministerial room as one succeeded another. By the end of five years I was by far the oldest inhabitant and I could hardly refrain from the attitude of a benevolent uncle towards rather wayward and almost ephemeral nephews and nieces.

What a zealous Minister would have seen 'on the shop-floor' at one of the monthly meetings of the UGC would have been the tiny tip of a substantial iceberg of continuous and unspectacular hard work. We equipped ourselves with a solar system of expert sub-committees, medical, agricultural, technological, the lot. They, and the Committee, spent a great deal of time visiting universities for formal or informal discussions. The formal ones, full-dress visits by the whole Committee, were direly designated 'Visitations'. I have seen these occasions referred to in print as a 'stately minuet'. I fancy that if the writer who so described them had ever been present at one he would have found it more like a gallop. At each university we saw deputations from the Senate, the non-professional staff, wardens of halls of residence, representatives of the Welfare and Counselling services, and officers of the Students' Union. At the end of it all it was the duty of the Chairman of the UGC to address the Council of

With the Macmillans at Delphi during a Swan's
Hellenic Cruise, 1965

With Denys Haynes, Keeper of Greek and Roman Antiquities, in the Duveen Gallery at the British Museum, 1971

The Queen at the opening of the Tutankhamun Exhibition, 1972, with Eiddon Edwards, Humphrey Trevelyan, the (then) Egyptian Ambassador H. E. Kamal ed-Din Rifaat and Dr Gamal ed-Din Mukhtar, then Director of the Egyptian Antiquities Service

the university, partly to give them a wider picture of the university world as a whole and partly to convey to them the Committee's impression as a result of the conversations they had held. The purpose of these onerous and time-consuming excursions was not to make snap decisions in each place. It was twofold: to enable each element in each university to meet members of the Committee face to face and say its piece man to man; and to enable members of the Committee to form a personal impression of each university, so that when its affairs came up for discussion there should be some first-hand evidence and experience in the mind and memory of each member of the Committee. It may sound – and it may have been – superficial and amateurish. But again it has to be remembered that the visitors themselves were academics, capable of judgments about colleagues in universities other than their own and familiar, in their own experience, with all the problems. And, as I knew from having endured Visitations before I inflicted them, it does a university no harm to have to stand back every now and then from its day-to-day affairs and give an account of itself to knowledgeable enquirers.

These state occasions were not without their lighter moments. Once, when the Committee, peregrinating Yorkshire, found road transport more convenient than the railway, its hired minibus stopped for lunch at a wayside hotel. Its highly respectable Secretary dismounted for conversation with the landlord. 'Can't ta reead?' 'I don't think I quite understand.' 'What does it say up theear?' 'Er, well, what?' 'Nooa buses ner cooaches.' And the cream of the academic world had to find its lunch elsewhere.

Students' Unions often provided unintended enjoyment. Where-ever we went, and whatever the local scandals to which they wished to call our attention, there were invariably two items in the Unions' representations. First, students' grants were grossly inadequate. The answer to that one was easy – the UGC was not responsible for students' grants. Secondly, the amount of provision for the parking of students' cars was grossly inadequate. It never seemed to occur to any of them that there was any sort of inconsistency between these two complaints.

Visitations were one way of keeping in touch with our consti-tuents. There were many others. Practically every day one vice-chancellor or another came to see me about something or other; registrars and finance officers came to Belgrave Square (later to Park

Crescent) to talk about building projects or financial worries with the Committee's officials. And, on the other front, there were sessions at the Department, meetings with the research councils – and plenty of Parliamentary Questions. Never, I think, was responsibility for the deployment of so much public money carried by so few.

All this must sound very unacademic and very much concerned with mere money. But money, getting it and allocating it to what we thought the best advantage, was our job. The UGC does not run the universities: it tries to provide them with the money to run themselves. There were non-financial moments. Installations of new chancellors (and there were a good many of them in the coming-to-be of so many universities), conferences with Commonwealth universities, dinner parties at No. 10, and visitors from all over the world who wanted to know how this strange British institution worked. It was not easy to explain; still less easy was it to transplant to other soils and foreign climates. Essentially the UGC is Mr Facing-both-ways, or, less disreputably, Janus. Its whole place in the system of things depends on a triangular relationship of trust and confidence between the three partners, the universities, the Government, and the UGC; and it is very difficult to codify a web of gossamer. I do not think that our method of financing universities is perfect. But I do profoundly believe that it is better than any other that anybody else has yet devised anywhere else in the world.

10

The British Museum
[1968]

My first reaction was open-mouthed incredulity. I was nearing the end of my five-year stint at the University Grants Committee when the Powers That Be invited me to go over and see him in Whitehall. Would I like to go on for another five years at the UGC? Thank you very much for the implied confidence, but no. Why not? Because I thought it was a mistake that an institution like the UGC should come to be identified with one individual. Then what about going on year by year until I was tired of it? No, thank you. Why not? Because the indeterminacy of the tenure would inevitably produce an air of uncertainty in the university world. Well then, what? Go away into the country and read a book, which I had not done in any serious way for twenty years. Oh no, I was certainly not going to be allowed to do that.

And then it came – the suggestion that I might go and be Director of the British Museum for five years. When I had closed my mouth and taken breath I began to produce all the obvious objections – I had never worked in a museum or library, I was no expert in any one of its manifold fields of activity, I knew nothing of its administration or finances, I should be regarded by all the museum world and (most important of all) by colleagues in the British Museum as an interloper and an impostor. Many of these objections were ingeniously turned into positive arguments for doing it. Eventually I was released, totally bewildered, with an injunction to think it over for a few days and come back with an answer, preferably an affirmative one, then.

The more I brooded the more attractive the idea came to be. All that I had said in that Whitehall room was true. But other factors began to come in. I did not particularly want to stop working at the age of sixty-two; I thought perhaps I might have one last job in me, and an entirely fresh field of activity might be just the thing. I began to be attracted by the thought of renewing direct personal involvement in the life of a single scholarly community. The UGC had indeed been involved with the university communities, but in a second-remove sort of way. My ignorance of the Museum's specialisms began to weigh less heavily; as a vice-chancellor I had not been expected to know more about nuclear physics or agricultural chemistry than the professors of these subjects – and why should the same not be true of Western Asiatic Antiquities or Ethnography? It was obviously a highly responsible job, in an institution of world-wide reputation and prestige, and if the Powers That Be thought I could do it, it was not for me to chicken out, especially as it had been made clear to me that there were likely to be considerable problems, institutional, administrative and indeed political, over the next five years.

For several days we swithered. We did not want to leave the attractive house in Chelsea we had bought when I left Reading to go to the UGC. On the other hand, the Director's Residence, in which we should be required to live, was as near to the lodgings of a head of an Oxford college as we should now be likely to reach. We had disposed of a good deal of furniture (and fifteen hundred books) in the move from Vice-Chancellor's Lodge to a domestic house in Chelsea: how were we to furnish a vast official residence again? The attractions of living on our own, with a Square garden in front of us and congenial neighbours, had grown on us over our five years there. On the other hand, the attractions of 'living over the shop', especially such a majestic shop, were not to be sneezed at. But at the end of the day the decision had to be made. It was; so I went back to Whitehall and said 'Yes'. There were important procedural steps to be taken. The appointment was not in the hands of Whitehall but of the Trustees of the British Museum; the function of Whitehall had been that of an intermediary. It was necessary also that the appointment should be approved by the Prime Minister. I could not leave the UGC immediately, so there had to be an interregnum at the Museum, but that presented no serious difficulty, since there was a distinguished and highly acceptable Keeper who could perfectly well keep the home fires burning until I arrived. My predecessor and his wife gave us every possible help. Eventually, in the summer of 1968 it was publicly announced that I was to go to the British Museum on January 1st, 1969.

Then the storm broke. Letters to *The Times* made all the expected points, with some violence. It was monstrous that somebody with no relevant experience of any kind should be planted in a highly specialised organisation like the British Museum. How could morale be maintained, either in the museum profession at large or in the British Museum itself, if this top job went to an outsider? It was disgraceful that this 'prestigious' appointment should be used as a sinecure for a senescent civil servant to enable him to clock up the necessary number of years to qualify for his pension. And so on. It should be said, and I record it with gratitude, that the British Museum itself took no part in these outbursts. On the contrary, the local Secretary of the First Division Association, representing Keepers and Assistant Keepers, took the trouble to write and assure me of their goodwill and loyalty. Our children took the news with more balanced irreverence: 'Oh well, we always knew you were a museum piece: now somebody else has found out as well.' Altogether, though, a pretty sticky start.

It was carried off by the determination and aplomb of the Chairman of the Trustees, David Eccles. He had decided that this was the right appointment for the British Museum at this particular stage, and he was not to be deflected. At a press conference he made his position clear; and I said that I was not at all surprised by the views that had been expressed – this was the third time in my life that similar things had been said, first when I went from being a don to being a headmaster, when the schoolmasters understandably protested at the presentation of a plum job to a young whipper-snapper from outside, and secondly, in reverse, when I moved from headmastering to being vice-chancellor of a university. So the professional protests this time were no novelty. It was not for me to say how far the misgivings expressed on the earlier occasions had been justified; two schools and one university seemed to have survived; would it not perhaps be more sensible all round if we set about proving the pudding by eating a bit of it instead of condemning it untasted? But for a week or two I did wonder if it might have been more comfortable to stay at the University Grants Committee.

Both the Trustees and the Department of the Environment were notably generous in the re-decoration and equipping of the Director's Residence – re-named by us the Director's House. There were delays in the completion of the necessary work; but waiting was worth it. Over the years, when we said we lived on the spot, people asked, intelligently, 'Oh, you have a flat there, do you?' and were surprised to be told that we had a five-storey house which occupied almost one-third of the south-western wing of the building. Some may have thought this an excessive allowance of space for a Director and his wife. But without it we could certainly not have carried out what we considered to be our duties in hospitality and entertainment. After each meeting of the Trustees we had a buffet lunch for them and Keepers and senior staff to the number of some forty bodies, and during the Tutankhamun Exhibition later on it was non-stop variety.

From the first the Museum was a fascinating place to work in. It had plenty of traditions, conventions, mythologies and taboos. But it seemed not to have much of a central administration. Indeed, there were many who thought that the less there was of that the better, on the assumption that the more there was of it the more constraints there would be on the people who actually did the Museum's work, in scholarship, publication, display, presentation and meeting the needs of the public. I, having been mistakenly labelled 'an administrator', (after all, I wasn't anything else, so I must be that) was suspected of all kinds of designs intended to impose the rigidity of a central bureaucracy on the essentially 'wind blowing where it listeth' freedom of the individual scholar.

That was not my idea or my intention. I am not by nature a bureaucrat. I had no wish to interfere in the proper internal autonomy of a Keeper in his Department – the analogy of a professor recurs – or to have views in his professional field. But there were two areas where some sort of contribution from the centre seemed to be not only possible but desirable. First, the very richness of the diversity of the Museum seemed to obscure its unity. In the famous phrase of a former Keeper, 'The British Museum is not one museum; it is twelve museums.' This is an admirable tribute to the importance and standing of each of the twelve Departments. But wide as the range was from Prints and Drawings to Western Asiatic Antiquities there must be at least some principles and practices accepted throughout the institution and some unity discernible in its multiform variety.

The second point follows from the first. 'The Director's Office', as the central administration was charmingly called, was regarded by practically everybody as a service department, dealing with house-keeping matters like establishments, accounts, maintenance, security, accommodation and so on. Fair enough, so it was. Perhaps it was really only a matter of nomenclature. If these various administrative affairs had been lumped together as 'Common Services' I should have minded less. But when a minor squabble occurred, as from time to time it was bound to do, between the accounts branch and a Department, I felt, perhaps over-sensitively, that it was rather hard that this should be charged up against the Director's Office and therefore indirectly against the Director. It all seemed symbolic of a disjunction, if not an antagonism, between the Departments, who desired and used these services, and the Director's Office, which, in the face of considerable financial difficulties, was not always able to provide them to the satisfaction of the consumer. One thing stood out a mile, that in these respects the Director's Office was seriously understaffed. This was not the general impression inside the Museum, where there was a natural suspicion of an ever-swelling central bureaucracy. But the fact was that over many years the complexities of running the Museum had imperceptibly increased. There were almost daily consultations, at all levels, with the Civil Service Department about staff appointments, with the Department of Education and Science, on whose Vote we were carried for salaries and wages, and with the Department of the Environment, who were responsible for the fabric, maintenance and structural services. Security services were increasingly complex and sophisti-cated. Financial arrangements (with VAT as the last straw) demanded more and more expert attention. We needed considerable strength-ening at the level of middle management if we were to carry out our obligations to our colleagues in the Departments.

The other serious problem seemed to be on a different level. There seemed to be no central synoptic organ with responsibility for reviewing or proposing policy for the Museum as a whole, as distinct from the Departments. Rightly or wrongly I felt it my business to be concerned with the unity of the Museum, in the belief that it, as a great international institution, was something more than the sum of its parts, distinguished as each of these was. So I thought it was at any rate part of my job to build up something at the centre which should not only serve the Departments in the nuts-and-bolts sense but should also be able to help and advise the Trustees in matters of general policy, and be able to hold up the Museum's end in dealings with government departments – and all this without giving any ground for an 'us-and-them' antithesis in any of these fields of activity. It was not wholly different, in my picture of it, from being vice-chancellor of a university, especially in this business of whole-and-parts and in relationships with colleagues. I had a lot to learn.

The analogy with a university was not entirely groundless. But analogies are most instructive and significant at the point where they break down. And so it was here. The first difference between the British Museum and a university is a constitutional one. As a general rule there are in a university two major legislative bodies, a Senate and a Council. The former consists entirely of academics, and in academic matters is autonomous and supreme. The latter consists for the most part of distinguished 'lay' persons from outside the university and has wider responsibilities, including finance and continuing trusteeship. The vital link between the two bodies is provided by the presence on the Council of some members of the Senate, either elected by their academic colleagues or enjoying membership of the Council by virtue of holding the office of Dean or Pro-Vice-Chancellor or whatever. In the Museum there was no such link. In so far as the Keepers and Assistant Keepers as a body could be equated with the Senate of a university and the Trustees with its Council, the constitutional difference from a university was that there were no Keepers included in the body of Trustees. This is not to say that there were no links between Trustees and Keepers. There were. But for the most part they were links, often very close, between individual Trustees and individual Keepers: they were not constitutional connections between two corporate bodies.

Indeed, there was no corporate body of Keepers. There were Keepers' Meetings, every five or six weeks, chaired by the Director. But they were not legislative, as meetings of a university Senate are for the university's academic affairs. Rather, they were opportunities for exchanges of views and information, sometimes leading to representations to be made on behalf of the Keepers by the Director to the Trustees. To a new Director, especially one inexperienced in the Museum's affairs, they were invaluable. But they had no official or constitutional standing. I am not arguing whether or not they should have. I am only saying that the analogy between the Museum and a university is incomplete.

There was one respect in which the parallel with a university was very close. Just as in a university professors and lecturers are the guarantors of academic standards, so in the British Museum Keepers and their Assistant Keeper colleagues are the guardians of the standards of scholarship without which the whole fabric and frame of the institution would crumble and fade. It is not always realised that rigorous, patient, dedicated scholarship is the fundamental rock on which the British Museum is built. There is a continuous stream of books, learned articles and exhibition catalogues, on any topic from Maya jades to Greek and Roman pottery lamps, or Egyptian painting to early autograph albums. The primary material for these publications is a Department's collection, and the wise Keeper encourages his junior colleagues towards an individual specialisation which may lead to an international reputation.

It follows that the recruitment of the right young men and women is of the first importance; and immense care is taken by all concerned when vacancies arise. Normally the Museum gets its pick of the annual university output in the relevant subject; the chief difficulty is that with small Departments and highly specialised staff these vacancies occur infrequently, so that potentially good people go elsewhere simply because there is not a job available at the right moment. I tried to encourage more interchange of staff between the Museum and the universities, partly to give to individuals a wider experience than the Museum could by itself provide, partly to provide us with outposts in the universities. But practical problems like salary structures and career prospects made it difficult to go as far as I would have liked.

Each Keeper ran his Department in his own idiosyncratic style. There was a long tradition of autocratic autonomy, mellowed in more modern days by a personal informality which would have made top-hatted predecessors blanch and blench. Some of them were more businesslike than others; some had more of a flair than others about new acquisitions; some were more enterprising than others in mounting temporary exhibitions to celebrate a centenary or a new excavation; some were more interested than others in the techniques of conservation or display. But without exception they were devoted to the place, quietly proud of their contribution to it, determined, each of them, that his own Department should be the fairest jewel in the crown of the most distinguished museum in the world. Inevitably, I had my moments of impatience and even occasional exasperation; but they were a good lot.

The other major constitutional issue ought perhaps rather to be called administrative – but that is not a word or a concept that I am very fond of. It concerned the manner in which the Trustees' business was actually conducted. There are twenty-five Trustees of the British Museum, every single one of whom is a person of national, often international, standing. Many of them are world experts in one or other of the areas of the Museum's activities. They meet nine or ten times a year, on Saturday mornings. They are more regular in their attendance than the members of any other body I have ever known; the average turn-out is twenty or twenty-one, and the others are either ill or abroad.

The actual business presented to a Trustees' meeting was, in my time at any rate, a remarkable mixture. There were reports from the departmental committees which had met since the last meeting, each presented by its chairman and each thoroughly discussed. There were lists of purchases proposed by Keepers, and each of these was debated, often at length. There were requests for loans, from other museums and galleries for exhibitions there. (It is, incidentally, quite untrue, though widely believed, that the British Museum is un-generous in lending. Stung one day by this accusation I circulated to each Keeper an immediate request for the insurance value of the objects in his Department out on loan on that day. The total was over £900,000.) There might be proposals for radical re-organisation of the Publications Department or the Education Service. There might be appointments to confirm. There might, very occasionally, be losses to report. There were always items from the Buildings Committee, suggesting ever more ingenious ways of utilising to the full our permanently cramped accommodation. There might be discussion of more effective ways of using our private Trust income, not least that from the estate of George Bernard Shaw. There were always gifts to be reported – and subsequently acknowledged to the donors by the Director on expensive paper in traditional form and almost eighteenth-century language. To this sort of rag-bag, on Saturday mornings ten times a year, twenty extremely distinguished persons gave their time, their interest, and their judgement.

The problem was how most effectively to harness all this experience, wisdom and devotion to the service of the Museum. There was a battery of committees, with terms of reference not always very clearly defined. Some were what might be called departmental committees, each of which took under its wing a group of related departments; others, like the committees on Buildings or Publications, were trans-departmental. The former were, in principle, advisory: the latter were executive. The real problem, and I suppose it is inescapable (and perhaps insoluble) in a place like the British Museum, was to be sure of the extent to which the departmental committees remained advisory and did not imperceptibly, and almost inadvertently, become executive. Each of them made recommendations to the Trustees. Each of them had close to its heart the interests of the group of departments with which it was concerned. These sets of interests, naturally enough, did not always coincide. In that event it was for the Trustees to adjudicate. But if the question was, for instance, about re-allocation of gallery space, it was not easy for the Trustees as a whole to decide between two of their colleagues, each a world-renowned figure, when as chairmen of committees they expressed diametrically opposite views with equal authority and passion.

It did not help that the supreme body, the Trustees, met much more frequently than did the subsidiary bodies, the committees. So it could happen, and did, that the Trustees as a body took decisions, of an executive kind, as a body of first instance, without the opportunity of having before it advice from its relevant committees. I wondered sometimes if the actual number of Trustees, as laid down in the British Museum Act of 1963, was the right number for doing business. If the number had been substantially bigger, it would have been necessary to have a comparatively small Executive Committee to get on with the job: if the number had been twelve or fifteen then very little delegation to committees would have been necessary. Twenty-five sometimes seemed to be just the wrong number, especially when they met at a vast oblong table in a room which acoustically must be one of the worst in London. Nobody could have wished, heaven knows, to get rid of any of the twenty-five, who individually and collectively set and maintained a magnificent standard of public service. But it might have been better not to have just that number from the start.

There was one other problem, arising partly from the numerical size of the Trustees' body and partly from the scholarly interests and enthusiasms of each member of it. It must be very hard for persons of such distinction in a particular field so to widen their focus as to include other areas of the Museum's activities with equal involvement. If you are a world-expert in the literature of the Big-endians (I deliberately take a fictitious example) and passionately devoted to the British Museum's collection of it, it cannot be easy to recognise a colleague's comparable zeal for the sculpture of the early Moon-age and the Museum's collection of that. There must be a danger, in such circumstances, that enthusiasm for the part may obscure proper attention to the welfare of the whole. And it was the welfare of the whole which I took to be my prime responsibility.

However all this may be – and none of it implies any criticism whatever of any individuals – it was all in the background, not the foreground, of daily life. And that foreground was pretty full, of people and events. There were some 1,700 persons in the employ of the Trustees; and there were rather more than 2,000,000 visitors a year to the Museum, or, more accurately, rather more than 2,000,000 visits – nobody knows how many visits each visitor makes. It was not the case that the Director sat Olympianly aloof, thinking beautiful thoughts and meditating high policy, or enjoying a sinecure. Every time the telephone rang it might be an ambassador arranging a visit by his head of State, or an infuriated Reader protesting about the delay in the arrival of his books, or a newspaper investigating a report that a priceless manuscript had been stolen, or a Trustee wanting to discuss the business for next Saturday's meeting, or somebody wanting the British Museum (Natural History), or the director of a museum in the United States who would be passing through London next day. The day's correspondence, delivered almost continuously by the most efficient internal messenger service in London, reflected a similar range of involvement.

But all this is still, relatively, in the background. The foreground, the front line, was at the Front Gate, in the Forecourt, in the Front

Hall, and in the galleries. And in all those areas the men in the front line were the warders. My admiration for them is boundless and my debt to them immeasurable. I think that in many ways the men on the Front Gate have the stickiest time of all. They have to explain to a group of foreign visitors that the Museum is not open on Good Friday; that the best way from here to the National Gallery is so-and-so, unless you dislike the Underground, in which case it is such-and-such; that the Forecourt is not there for free parking while you do your shopping; that although there is, deliberately, not a notice saying so, visitors are requested not to use the lawns as places for running races or for their afternoon nap. They are the people who give to visitors coming for the first time their first impression of the British Museum, and they are a splendid company of public relations officers. Just every now and then, but very rarely, one will blow his top after continued interrogation from the one visitor in ten thousand who is determined to be awkward. But their patience, good humour, helpfulness and loyalty are one of my warmest recollections.

Their colleagues inside the building will, of course, be jealous of what I have just said. Far be it from me to foment dissensions within the ranks of this splendid body of men. They all have their problems, whatever their station; it simply is the case that the first impression on the public is given by the 'front men'. And that first impression is amply confirmed inside the building itself. There are school-children to be shepherded, foreign tourists to be informed, disabled visitors to be helped. And in their minds all the time is the security of the collections, the possibility that at any moment some lunatic may again attack the Portland Vase or throw red paint over the Elgin Marbles. Their function is not simply ornamental, still less otiose. The measure of their success is the remarkable rarity of untoward incidents.

There were the hundreds of others beavering away – some more assiduously than others – in their respective contributions to the day-to-day running of the place. Telephone-girls, sales-counter staff, executive officers, typists, carpenters, locksmiths, housemaids – yes, that is what they were officially called – and the messengers in perpetual motion. From time to time there were rumblings from one or other of the half-dozen professional associations or trade unions represented in the Museum. But from what was said of other organisations, for instance by Trustees who were involved in productive industry or even in universities, we got off comparatively lightly. It often seemed that the real problem for many of the staff was the conflict which sometimes arose for them between proper loyalty to their unions and their deep and affectionate loyalty to the Museum. Anyhow, recollected in tranquillity, it might have been a great deal worse.

Among all these colleagues the three of whom I saw most were the Deputy Director, Maysie Webb, the Secretary to the Museum, Bentley Bridgewater, and my personal secretary, Enid Roberts. Maysie Webb had come to the Museum, six months before my own arrival, from the National Reference Library of Science and Invention, into which she had transformed the former Patent Office Library. She had spent practically all her working life in libraries of one kind or another, chiefly in the context of science and information, and I often wondered what she made of my intrusion into a world which was as familiar to her as it was unfamiliar to me. In the newly-created post of Assistant Director to which she came she quickly established herself and by the time I arrived she had pretty clear and forceful ideas of what there was to be done. We did not always see exactly eye to eye (whatever that means), but I quickly came to respect her energy, her pertinacity and her total devotion to the Museum. No, 'total devotion' is misleading in two respects. She had deep interests in other things, from bird-watching to chess and from electrical machines to gardening. And her devotion was to her ideals for the Museum, towards the realisation of which she laboured with deep and unselfish persistence.

Bentley Bridgewater was a very different cup of tea. He had spent his whole working life in the British Museum, except for a wartime interlude at Bletchley. In many respects he was the incarnation of 'the Museum man', civilised, urbane, articulate, a member of The Athenaeum. His working hours did not always coincide with those of the rest of us; and a fair amount of his time was spent on the telephone. But to me he was invaluable, increasingly as a personal friend, but from the start as a walking encyclopedia of the Museum, its personalities, its history, its traditions, its mythologies – all narrated, when the occasion arose, with almost continental fluency. Doubtless I dropped a fair number of bricks: there would have been many more without him. It was never exactly clear to me what the

Secretary's job was, apart from the quite substantial business of servicing Trustees and their committees with papers and keeping their minutes. But he had certainly made a distinctive personal niche for himself, and the vast concourse of staff at his farewell party was an outward and visible sign of the affection felt for him by every sort and condition of his colleagues.

Enid Roberts, whom I should never have presumed to address by her Christian name while I was still there, is that increasingly rare pearl of untold price, a genuinely and utterly loyal personal secretary. After a long journey in to work she arrived at ten minutes to nine precisely, having walked, at immense speed, from Charing Cross station. As often as not she brought something for me from her garden, where she and her husband must have worked as long hours as she did in Bloomsbury. In one sense she was of 'the old school', in her blistering scorn for anybody she regarded as working less than flat out the whole day, as she instinctively did herself. In another sense she was very much with it, in the kind of story she would tell me when she thought she knew me well enough. She typed like a machine-gun, her telephone manners were impeccable, and she seemed to know in advance how I should react to practically anything. She was a figure in the Museum in her own right, not at all because she asserted herself or put on airs as the boss's secretary, but because everybody knew that they could trust her absolutely and that she was a person of deep and personal considerateness and unsentimental kindness, especially if there was a youngster who was under the weather or who thought she had been unjustly treated. People like her don't grow on trees, not even in her own garden.

These three were my closest daily associates, together with the Chairman of the Trustees. I suspected that David Eccles had been mainly responsible for my appointment. I suspected also that he had probably had to put up with a fair amount of criticism about it. If so, he loyally resisted it and never passed it on to me. He was deeply interested and personally involved in all the Museum's affairs and at that time it was the main outlet for his active mind and his apparently unlimited energy. Every now and then it was a little unclear what the respective functions of the Chairman and the Director were, and I was sometimes uncertain whether I was Permanent Secretary to a Minister or Managing Director of a company. I was, of course, neither; nor was I any longer a headmaster or a vice-chancellor or Chairman of the UGC, but Director of the British Museum, with a forceful and energetic Chairman in intimate daily touch with its affairs. It is not altogether easy to work out a new relationship of this kind when you are well into your sixties; but between us we made it work, though I guess it would have been difficult for a third party to codify and write down exactly who did what. His successor, Humphrey Trevelyan, was different indeed in temperament but equally assiduous in his devotion to the Museum and all it stood for. The world at large never realises how much time and energy such distinguished people freely and spontaneously give to the concerns of such places as the British Museum, without any sort of public recognition or reward – or, indeed, any kind of expectation of it.

There were two questions which I was asked roughly twice a week, by somebody or other. My replies were (and are) my own; they bind neither the Trustees nor the Keepers – still less my successor. The first was: 'Is it true that what you have on public display is only one-tenth of what the Museum possesses, the rest being inaccessibly stacked in the cellars?' The first, rather pedantic, answer was that the answer depended on which Department you were talking about, because the facts differed enormously from one Department to another. But in essence the answer, my answer, was something like this. 'Yes, of course it is true that what is on public display is only a small proportion of the collections of each Department. Do you remember what a museum was like in my (and your) youth? You went into a dark room with cupboards along the walls, containing, behind unwashed glass doors, a row of Greek pots standing shoulder to shoulder like guardsmen. When you (or I) had walked past them we had never seen a Greek vase: we had a confused smudged collective blur of 'Greek pot'. Modern methods of display are quite different. If you can, you make it possible for a three-dimensional object, like a Greek vase, to be seen from front, side and back. You can now walk all round the Caryatid from the Erectheum and see how her hair-style looks from behind. Obviously, this means that each object will need more space in a gallery. Therefore there are fewer objects on permanent public display. But this does not mean that all the rest are lost in cobwebbed cellars, surrounded by emaciated cats. They are all numbered, registered and catalogued; and if you want to see any of them all you have to do is ask the Keeper. And I'll tell you this. If I had all the space in the world I would never dream of putting on exhibition 300,000 pieces of Babylonian cuneiform tablet each one inch square, or our thousands of apparently identical assegais from West Africa.'

The second question went nearer to fundamentals. It was, 'Who (or what) is the British Museum for? Is it for the scholar or for the British public?' I always refused to accept a disjunction, still less an antithesis, between the scholar and the public. The Museum existed, I maintained, to serve a whole spectrum of people. At one end were our own resident scholars, the Keepers; then there were their colleagues from all the countries of the world, working with them, or on their own, with our collections; then there were the individual scholars, writing their books on Chinese jade or Boeotian pottery; then there were those who were researching on behalf of novelists who wanted to get their facts right; then there were the script-writers for television or radio programmes; then there was the Great British Public; and then there were their children, by no means the least important element in our clientele. We existed to serve all these. Obviously, there would from time to time be conflicts between the very different needs of these very various categories; it was our business to try to ensure that all the needs of all of them were, so far as in us lay, met. In fact I had by now discovered that children were bringing their parents to the Museum, rather than the other way round.

Out of this sort of question arose my first major policy paper for the Trustees. The occasion was a discussion about our acquisitions policy. The practice was that each Keeper had an annual grant for what might be called run of the mill acquisitions for his Department, the Trustees reserving in their own discretion a substantial proportion of the annual acquisitions grant from the Government for major purchases, irrespective of Department. The procedure was that before each Trustees' meeting Keepers who had major purchases in mind displayed the objects in the Board Room, so that the Trustees should be able to see and touch the pieces about which they were required to adjudicate. After half a dozen meetings I began to wonder what the principles were behind the Trustees' judgments. I sometimes heard somebody say, 'That's lovely, we must have it;' or, alternatively, 'We can't buy that tatty thing.' Greatly daring, I put forward the view that the primary function or duty of the British Museum was not aesthetic but historical. We were not primarily concerned with beautiful things – there were other museums and galleries which were – or with items of individual aesthetic appeal: our function was primarily historical. If pressed, I would say – and I said so after consultation with Keepers – that if I had to express the fundamental function of the British Museum, as distinct from other museums and galleries, it would be in the rather pompous and poly-syllabic phrase that we were there to represent the documentation of human achievement. It did not matter whether the documents were statues of Buddha or the Elgin Marbles or the Lindisfarne Gospels or the manuscript of *Alice's Adventures Underground*; they were all documents, and that was what we were here to provide, for scholars and for anybody who was interested. It happened, by the grace of God or creative evolution, that some of these documents were beautiful to look at. But that, from our point of view, was an uncovenanted benefit, not a primary incentive to acquisition. This doctrine was not totally acceptable (I had never supposed it would be) but at least the presentation of it made the Trustees aware that it would be a good thing if they had a policy and not just a moment-by-moment reaction to individual objects presented for their acceptance. The sensible outcome was that Departments were required to formulate their own particular acquisitions policies, which, quite properly, differed *inter se*.

The presence of children in the Museum was a constant joy. They arrived by the coach-load, on school parties, and they poured out with plenty of cheerful noise – after all, a morning in the British Museum couldn't be worse than an ordinary morning in school, could it? The benefit they got from it depended very largely on how much preparation and briefing they had had beforehand. Left to themselves they would make inexorably for the Egyptian mummies: there is a curious necrophily about the young which I do not claim to understand. In the vast majority of cases they came well instructed and full of zeal to fill in their questionnaires; only about once in six months did I have to turn headmaster and go on the rampage about banana skins thrown from coaches on to the lawns or boisterous races being run over the hundred-yard course of the King's Library. More characteristic, from both ends, is an event which concerned children and the late King of Sweden, a field archaeologist of distinction. He was, in his seventies, a regular visitor, in an entirely informal and un-regal way, as a practitioner visiting colleagues. I was with him one day in one of the Greek galleries, which had recently been re-arranged and was therefore of particular interest to him. In the gallery at the same time was a score of children, in grey stockings and pink blazers, with a devoted young mistress in charge. In their enthusiasm to fill in their question-sheets these youngsters kept getting between the King and the cases he was looking at. After repeated interpositions I said, 'Don't you think, sir, I might ask this nice girl to take her flock off to look at something else, so that we can look at this case and they can come back when you have seen it?' 'Certainly not,' said His Majesty, 'if more people of my age saw more young people of that age enjoying themselves in that way, more people of my age would be a great deal happier than they are.' On his next visit, over a quiet drink, I told him that I had been dining out on this judgment of his. He disclaimed any recollection of it. When I narrated it he said, 'That's much too clever for me; you must have made it up.' Which goes to confirm the crack about His late Majesty, that he had a mind above his station.

The joy of the British Museum was this unique (and I use the adjective in full knowledge of its unique meaning) combination of attributes. At one and the same time it could be, as it was, described as a postgraduate university; and it could be, and was, a place which two million ordinary people visited each year. Living on the spot, we were daily aware of this variety of functions. We might have lunching with us a scholar (for instance, Arnold Toynbee hard at work on his new speciality), while sitting on our front doorsteps was a Japanese visitor eating his sandwiches in smiling disregard of any 'Private' notices, and, simultaneously, a coach-load of school-children from practically anywhere in Britain being eyed with disapproval by a coach-load of courier-conducted visitors from the United States or Düsseldorf.

The most 'public' event of my time at the Museum was, I suppose, the Tutankhamun Exhibition. Contrary to general belief, the purpose of the Exhibition was not to make money for the Museum. The Egyptian Government generously allowed these treasures to leave Cairo and visit London in order first, that the British public might have an opportunity of seeing them; secondly, that money might be raised for the UNESCO enterprise of moving the temples of Philae to higher ground in order to save them from being submerged by the Nile. Both purposes were fulfilled, to the extent that 1,656,000 people saw them (on the assumption, no doubt fallacious, that nobody came twice), and that a cheque for over £650,000 was handed to the Egyptian Ambassador for 'onward transmission'. The British Museum did not pocket a penny.

Years of negotiation had preceded the official opening of the Exhibition by Her Majesty the Queen on March 29th, 1972. These were conducted at ambassadorial level in the two countries, and successive ambassadors, at both ends, gave of their time and interest far beyond the call of duty. It was a great help that Humphrey Trevelyan, the Chairman of our Trustees, had himself some years before been our ambassador in Cairo, and that Eiddon Edwards, our Keeper of Egyptian Antiquities, was deeply respected and totally trusted by the authorities of the Cairo Museum. There were disappointing setbacks and delays, some of them arising from political changes in Cairo. But eventually the great good news came that the agreement between the governments had been signed and that the way was now clear for me to sign the operational agreement with the Cairo Museum.

It was then that, in one sense, the fun began. We had to arrange for an expert team to go out and co-operate with the Cairo Museum in the actual packing of these priceless pieces. There was no question of insurance, but a governmental indemnity against loss or damage had to be arranged. The actual transporting of these fragile objects had to be organised with due regard to security, secrecy and temperature control. A cargo of this kind, especially at a time of turbulence and tension in the Middle East, would present a glorious opportunity for hi-jacking or sabotage; so we spread the risk by using three separate aircraft on three separate days. With the unlimited co-operation of the RAF, BOAC and the government departments concerned, it was all organised. It can now be thankfully recorded that neither on the journeys here and back nor during the Exhibition itself was any object lost or damaged.

Meanwhile, inside the British Museum itself preparations continued. We could never have found room for such an exhibition had we not just decided to move the Department of Ethnography out to a new home in Burlington Gardens. So its galleries, upstairs in the

East Wing, were available; and our young Exhibitions Officer, Margaret Hall, produced a brilliant plan which was both economical in space – it had to be – and dramatic in impact. We had no idea how many people would come. Our only evidence was what had happened when Tutankhamun had visited Paris some years before. But it seemed probable that we should have to cope with a considerable influx of visitors over and above our normal numbers. We were determined that so far as was humanly possible the disruption to our normal services should be kept to the minimum. So we had to recruit additional temporary staff, security men, catalogue sellers, cloakroom attendants, booking clerks, and, eventually, all the additional secretaries and telephone operators needed to deal with interminable correspondence and urgent requests.

All this cost money. The Department of the Environment were extremely generous and wholly co-operative in rushing through the necessary structural alterations to the galleries and laying on the essential services. But there had to be cash as well, and ready cash is a commodity of which the British Museum has very little. We were saved by a spontaneous piece of imaginative enterprise on the part of Denis Hamilton, Editor-in-chief of Times Newspapers, who had lately become a Trustee of the British Museum. He offered joint sponsorship by the *Sunday Times*, to meet expenses which could not properly be met from governmental sources and to relieve us of the administrative and organisational problems which would almost inevitably overwhelm our hard-pressed regular staff. For their financial backing of the Exhibition and for their expert help in the running of the business side of it we, and all those who visited it, owed a great deal to Times Newspapers.

Nevertheless, we had plenty of headaches. The first was almost comical. After the most stringent, and highly successful, security arrangements the first van-load arrived at Great Russell Street in the middle of a dark, wet, windy night. The van would just have been able to turn in at the south-west gate if there had not been a car parked on the south side of the street just where the van driver wanted to go to make the sharp turn in. While he tried time after time to swing his precious cargo into harbour the impatient traffic built up behind him – a great deal of traffic goes along Great Russell Street all through the night – and the secrecy of the operation would have gone up in smoke if anybody had guessed what the van contained. The deadlock was broken by four valiant policemen who lifted the car bodily on to the pavement until Tut had been safely delivered and then lifted it back again to its parking place.

There were, of course, plenty of bomb scares. We got used to them; our security officers and the ever-helpful police acquired a sixth sense in distinguishing serious ones from frivolous ones. But there was an occasion when the Director of the British Museum, for the first time in recorded history, stood on the steps with a megaphone and explained to fifteen hundred people waiting in the forecourt that the reason why they had been stationary for an hour was that a serious bomb threat had been made and although we were sorry to have kept them waiting we should have been sorrier still if they had been let in and blown to bits. This message, duly repeated by the Director to those who were queueing in the street, was received with murmurs of agreement and even with mild applause. People don't mind queueing, provided that the queue moves. If it does not they want to know why, and they have every right to be told.

There are endless stories of the good nature and honest fairness of the Great British Public during their hours of queueing. A remarkable neighbourliness developed, and awkwardnesses over all the months were in single figures. Two particular incidents are perhaps worth recording. A young foreign diplomat at one of the embassies told me at dinner afterwards that he had queued three times to get in. I expressed sympathy. He replied that the first time he had so much enjoyed the experience and the friendliness of his fellow-waiters that he had gone twice more just to queue and improve his conversational English. The other concerns two ladies who had almost reached the entrance to the tomb when they discovered that they had no tickets. The attendant warder asked them to stand aside from the queue, told me of the difficulty and suggested that I might have a word with them. I approached them and said I understood there was a problem. Yes, said one; they came from San Francisco and had been in London for ten days; they had been waiting for a long time and she had had to visit (what she called) the toilet; while she was there she had been through her handbag and torn up the counterfoils of the theatres they had been to during their visit; and she supposed she must have torn up the Tut tickets as well by mistake. It seemed to me that there was only one way to settle it. I marched them over to the queue and said, out loud, 'These ladies tell me that they bought some tickets downstairs – and indeed I can't see how they can have got as far as this without them. But as the result of a visit to the ladies' loo they no longer have any tickets. Can any of you identify them as having been near you in the queue so far?' Half a dozen hands went up immediately. 'Yes, they were just in front of us.' 'Yes, they were just behind us.' Totally confident of the fair-mindedness of the British queuer, I invited the ladies to resume what was agreed to be their place. They were overcome with gratitude. There was, however, I added, one small formality to be completed. What was that? That they must buy two more tickets. Gratitude faltered on their lips. Did that mean that they would have to go right back to the front door and start again? No, if they would give me a pound I would ask the warder to go down, get them the tickets and bring them back to them in the queue. But why? Because the warder on the turnstile had the sternest possible instructions to let nobody through without a ticket on any grounds whatsoever. They paid, the warder got their tickets and they entered the tomb. You can't be a headmaster for sixteen years without developing some sense of discipline, even over what happens in the ladies' loo.

There were streams of VIP's to whom special attention had to be paid, quite a few P's who thought they were VI, and quite a few genuinely distinguished persons who might reasonably have claimed special treatment but preferred to queue like everybody else. There will always, I suppose, be discussion and even controversy about the granting of any exceptions to normal rules. And as I watched the patient hundreds snaking round the forecourt after waiting out on the pavement and right round to Montague Place my heart hardened against would-be queue-jumpers or special pleaders. We had from the start had head-of-the-queue treatment for the disabled and the ailing aged; and we had reserved Monday mornings for organised and pre-booked school parties. But I saw no particular reason why other categories should, as categories, have special treatment. On the other hand, there were individuals who by reason of the ties of their work or national position could not, as a matter of the public good, be required to wait for an unpredictable time during their working hours. For these we evolved a 'nine a.m.' procedure. They came at nine o'clock in the morning, so that they could be sure of being through the exhibition in an hour, and I was not retarding the movement of the queue, since the head of the queue was not due to be admitted until ten o'clock. There was a further advantage for the distinguished persons who came at nine a.m. – and many of them were very distinguished indeed – that they were personally conducted round the Exhibition by Eiddon Edwards, our Keeper of Egyptian Antiquities and the man primarily responsible for the whole project. Day after day, week after week, for nine months, he did his nine a.m. tour and his exposition was just as fresh at the end of the Exhibition as it had been at the beginning.

While all this was going on the daily activities of the rest of the Museum had to be carried on as normally as might be. Obviously there were inconveniences and minor disruptions. But apart altogether from the two avowed purposes of the Exhibition there can be no doubt that there was a considerable spin-off for the Museum. Tens of thousands came to it for the first time, and thousands of them have been again since. And those who came lingered, either in the Egyptian galleries or in the King's Library, long after closing time. It was worth the headaches.

During this time the controversy about the British Library was bubbling up to the boil. It had long been a claim that one great advantage of the British Museum over comparable institutions elsewhere in the world was that it possessed both a wide range of objects and a wide range of books about them, all under the same roof. We never claimed that we were unique in this respect (that would have been hybristic and un-British), but we did, I think justifiably, claim that it was a great advantage to the scholarly user of the institution. But accessions, of objects and books, cannot go on indefinitely in a building which is on an island site and does not have elastic walls. The intake of books and other printed matter, through the Copyright Acts, gifts, purchases and exchanges, demanded additional shelving of two miles a year. That could not go on indefinitely, and 'out-housing', at Colindale, Woolwich and elsewhere, obviously reduced the aforesaid advantages. So something had to be done.

It would be tedious to recite the stages which had already been gone through. The Trustees of the British Museum had never objected in principle to the separation of the Library Departments from the Antiquities Departments. What they had maintained, with steady firmness, was that if this separation were to take place the

Library Departments, under their new name of 'British Library', should be housed as near as possible to the British Museum, preferably on a site on the south side of Great Russell Street, immediately opposite the Museum itself. There is a long history of recommendations, vacillations, government decisions, local authority objections, preservationist pressures and painstaking work by designated architects.

At last there was legislation, and the British Library Act of 1973 established a separate Board which should take under its wing all the national lending libraries and take over from the Trustees of the British Museum responsibility for the three Departments of Printed Books, Manuscripts, and Oriental Printed Books and Manuscripts. But there was no new building. On that rather important point – in practice, as distinct from constitutional theory or dogma, the only important one – controversy was renewed. So the books and manuscripts stayed in the same place, looked after by the same people, with nothing changed except that those people were now the servants of the British Library Board instead of being servants of the Trustees of the British Museum. In real life it was even more odd than that, because for a variety of reasons most of them opted to continue to be servants of the Trustees, seconded to the service of the Board.

All this involved hours of conversation and negotiation with the newly-appointed senior officers of the Board. There were notional frontiers to be drawn inside the one building, responsibilities for security to be agreed, recruitment procedures to be codified, even continued accessibility to the Museum's staff restaurant to be ratified. It worked, thanks to goodwill and common sense all round, though every now and then it creaked.

One day, somewhere, there will be a new building for the British Library (Reference Division). For the record, on July 1st, 1973, I ceased to be Principal Librarian and became, I suppose, the last person in history to hold the proud double title of Director and Principal Librarian of the British Museum.

Epilogue

I suppose the most shattering turning point of all (except for the ultimate one which awaits anything mortal) is retirement.

In prospect it represents everything that is desirable and attractive – time to read, paint, garden, stay with friends, take up some new form of voluntary service, travel, learn to play the violin. Above all, time.

In real life it is not quite like that. You pay your own postage, make your own telephone calls, and generally emerge from the cocoon of secretary-sheltered pampering into the cold windswept bus-queues of real life. And now that you are 'retired' dozens of people want to enlist you to do dozens of improbable things, because, forsooth, you now have 'plenty of time'. And so the prospect of blissful idleness and slippered ease reveals itself as a mirage.

But there are compensations. You do not have to do the things you do not want to do. A certain freedom of choice can be exercised, even about the time of getting up. And it is possible to go to bed, sometimes, without saying to yourself, 'Hell, I've got that man coming to see me at ten o'clock tomorrow morning.' There are more options open than there used to be; and when four-year-old grandchildren come on a visit they can be top and unchallenged priority for a whole day. You can go to lunch with friends in the country on a Tuesday or a Wednesday and not only on a Saturday or a Sunday. The wise man retains, indeed widens, his freedom of choice and activity, so that he can enjoy the *otium cum dignitate* to which a life of hard work has entitled him.

The fool lands himself with undertakings like being a chairman of committees – or writing a book.